libidos
and
life
lessons

libidos and life lessons

A memoir

MARIELLA PEARSON

THE
UNBOUND
PRESS

ISBN 978-1-913590-94-9 Paperback
ISBN 978-1-913590-95-6 Ebook

The Unbound Press
www.theunboundpress.com

Hey unbound one!

Welcome to this magical book brought to you by The Unbound Press.

At The Unbound Press we believe that when women write freely from the fullest expression of who they are, it can't help but activate a feeling of deep connection and transformation in others. When we come together, we become more and we're changing the world, one book at a time!

This book has been carefully crafted by both the author and publisher with the intention of inspiring you to move ever more deeply into who you truly are.

We hope that this book helps you to connect with your Unbound Self and that you feel called to pass it on to others who want to live a more fully expressed life.

With much love,
Nicola Humber

Founder of The Unbound Press
www.theunboundpress.com

For my friends

Who saw a story, where I saw a mess.

There are three sides to every story, mine, theirs and the truth. In this book there is purely my side of situations. This is my right as much as it is theirs to see it differently.

Dad, if you're reading this, please stop. If you are of any relation to me or still see me as an angelic blonde-haired blue-eyed angel, I suggest you stop reading before you're scarred for life.

Introduction

It's 1.04 am on a Saturday morning. I'm neither out living the high life, nor have I been out. I've been spending the last three hours tossing and turning, thinking of you. You, the people that are reading this, the people that may judge me, the people who may think I can't write and should have listened to the teachers growing up who were sure I wouldn't amount to anything.

It's a scary thing to lay yourself bare like I appear to be doing. Letting you into my innermost thoughts and secrets. Allowing you to judge me, to potentially ridicule me, but there is also the hope you'll identify with me.

When I started on this journey, I never expected to be here now, having started the process of publishing my own book. Even writing this sounds crazy – am I, in fact, in a dream? The little girl I was is so far from who I am today. She was shy, constantly terrified and didn't think she'd be worth anything. As the years went on, I presumed I would be dead before I got to my thirtieth birthday. But that wasn't to be. Instead, I'm here, having double-dropped a camomile tea bag into a cup of hot water, praying it will slip me into a drug-like oblivion and let me sleep.

I've spent my life wanting to be invisible, anonymous, and here I am doing the complete opposite. I'm putting the spotlight on myself, exposing myself for everyone to see. I think being strapped to a pole naked in my local market square would be preferable right now, as being judged on how we look is something we've all become accustomed to. Being judged on what goes on in our heads seems like a fairly new phenomenon.

How I got to this point, I'm not entirely sure. The little girl who played chess and struggled to make lasting friendships definitely didn't see herself publishing a book. Not only a book but one about herself and the painful journey into some sort of self-acceptance.

I guess I'm doing it for her. I was told when I was judging myself to look at a picture of me as a child and say the mean things I was thinking to her. Weirdly, I didn't find this so easy.

I'm doing this for the girl who thought she wasn't good enough, the girl who was always picked last for the netball team, the girl who didn't know how to be.

I'm doing this for all the little girls who think they can't. I'm here to prove they can.

THIS IS 28

Laugh or cry

Let's face it, you've got two options in life: you can laugh, or you can cry. Up until now, most of my twenty-something years have been the latter. I've always been a person that proclaims to want the quiet life, the sort that you see in the movies, living on a farm or similar, herding cattle and bringing up two point four children surrounded by a picket fence and an adoring husband. My reality is somewhat different.

At this moment in time, I'm sitting on my sofa, having just eaten nearly two tubs of Ben and Jerry's, the two most important men in my life to date. I've been spending the last couple of hours scrolling through social media; when I say scrolling, I actually mean stalking. That stalking came to an abrupt end when I accidentally liked a comment a girl left on an ex's photo. Was it the most recent one? Of course not! Which in turn led to me ringing one of my long-suffering friends to tell them about what a dick I'd been.

I've been blessed with what some close friends describe as chronic awkwardness and very little filter when it comes to talking to not only men but humans in general. I appear not to think an awful lot before I allow a thought to leave my mouth or slip through my digital fingers. How I've managed to coerce men into relationships with me, I'm not entirely sure. There have been some such men, however, who see through this immensely awkward young woman and are somehow charmed by what they see.

When in such relationships, I appear to change entirely. Your wish is my command, regardless of how I may feel. I become a habitual people-pleaser and an all-out pushover. So, some of the blame must fall at my feet for these failing romances. From being brutally truthful to being dishonest about almost everything. In my head, I'm thinking, 'Why on earth are they with me?' without ever asking myself, 'Do I want to be with them?'

And so, the cycle has continued. I've found myself in relationship after relationship without asking myself, 'Is this what you want?' The fear of being alone and unloved has always been too much for me to bear.

Bridget Jones's Diary was always the movie I would turn to. I could so identify with the woman that would sing and cry and think she was overweight, at NINE FUCKING STONE! I mean, someone have a word with the writer of that! Maybe I might find comfort in writing about my many failed romances and the constant chatter that goes on in my brain. Can it, after all, be as therapeutic as people say? Might I actually learn something? With no man currently here to take up my time or read my innermost thoughts, could this be the free therapy I so need?

The MENmoirs, maybe. All I know is where I am, in this moment, is not where I want to be or intend to be. I may look back and cringe whilst reading these scribblings of a lunatic, or I may be able to look back and see how far I've come.

Nothing in this life is certain; all that is certain is we only have one life.

What to look for in a man

For as long as I can remember, my taste in men has been questionable. Unfortunately, having not drunk for 11 years, I can no longer blame alcohol for these poor choices. Yes, you can somewhat survive dating and relationships sober, but it can cause complications. When I gave up drinking and everything that came with it, it was not so much a choice but my only option for survival. This, however, did not stop me from being attracted to the same men.

When I was 12 years old, I remember being stopped on the high street with one of my sisters; a student was doing some sort of survey and asking us who our celebrity crushes were. My sister was somewhat of a normal teenager and replied with Brad Pitt or Johnny Depp. At this tender age, my response was not quite so conventional: Ewan McGregor, but not just him as a person, specifically him in *Trainspotting*! I should have noticed the warning signs.

As my journey into adulthood continued, so did my love for all things that were distinctively bad for me. I found comfort in alcohol and drugs and men that looked like they could do with a good wash. The fake love you feel when you're on drugs is like nothing I've ever experienced again and something I seem to always be chasing. Where you feel like no one can touch you and you'd actually die for each other. This only continuing if I didn't run out of drugs or, in my case, end up in rehab, having just been branded by such a boyfriend. This now resembles a rather blurry tattoo, but at the time was a sign our love would last forever.

So now, being of a much clearer mind, my hope was that I would see through men's bullshit exteriors; unfortunately, this wasn't the case. This was unfortunate for not only me but my family around me. Having put so much into helping me turn a corner and not end up in a gutter somewhere covered in my own vomit, they no doubt hoped that I would somehow end up with a polo-playing farmer type to fit in with my want for the quiet life.

I feel, at this point, my glorious mother has to be mentioned. She, to me, is not like many of the conventional mothers out there. She is a beautiful woman – not only on the outside but on the inside too. She's had the joy of bringing up four daughters and two stepchildren who all happened to be going through puberty and teenage rebellion at the same time. My mother had a very different upbringing from me and my siblings. She was privileged enough to go to boarding school and, at times, had maids. She mingled with aristocracy; she had lots of opportunities to marry such men but chose love over lavish lifestyles. When speaking to one of my sister's friends about her new relationship choice, she told her the three most important things you need in a man: that they are kind, make you laugh, and are a good lover.

It appears that I need to focus more closely on these characteristics.

Prince Charming

I had finally made it to a year clean. The hope, I'm sure, was that I would find someone to match my new pure lifestyle. This was not the case. My first serious relationship being sober was, to be honest, an accident. Well, at least I never thought it would continue for the eight years that followed. He looked like the sort that would be doing all the things I used to do but appeared to be a lot more straight-edged.

Here I must add that my last boyfriend was a heroin addict living in a squat, so what I saw as straight was still pretty fucking blurry. He had tattoos and could charm any room he went into. The fact he didn't appear to take drugs and only drank actually made me think he was saint-like. I was taken in by this newfound 'Prince Charming'. My expectations of men at this point were still pretty low. He had never been to prison, didn't take drugs, and, to my knowledge, didn't deal them either.

I fell head over heels. I never thought I would find someone like him, and frankly didn't think I deserved any better. The fairy tale moved quickly, and after only a couple of months, we got a rescue dog together. Now, she was the true love of my life. She was the glue that stuck us together for many years. When things got tough, she was what kept me going.

Although no drugs or at least little drugs were taken by my new Prince Charming, alcohol was definitely his crutch. Many times when we were out, he would lose his temper at people for no apparent reason. I got into my first street scuffle with him as he thought some youths were making comments about my boobs. To start a fight with four blokes is probably not advisable, but with no inhibitions due to his intake of alcohol, to him, it was the only rational thing to do. I ended up grabbing one by the throat and pushing him up against a nearby shop front to try and stop him from going for my boyfriend. Not long after, the police were called, and the fight dispersed. I'd never felt so strongly towards anyone that I would actually involve myself like this. This, surprisingly, was the first of many such occasions.

I myself am a non-confrontational person. I avoid fights and everything that goes with them. But his anger often seemed to come from wanting to protect me. I had never had someone care for me like he did.

Our relationship came to an end one New Year's Eve. We had gone to a friend's family party; as usual, he drank too much and ended up leaving in a mood without telling me. I rang him, and he told me he had gone home, but I had the keys. In any other instance, I might have left him to stew, locked out of our flat, but knowing our beloved dog was no doubt getting wound up at the sound of him, I decided to go back to let him in.

His friend was staying at ours and so came back with me to greet someone whom I once felt so safe with. On arrival, I could hear my dog pining for this man she loved so dearly; a red mist had descended over him. All I could do was unlock the door. He went into our flat and continued to lose his temper. While I comforted our dog from his rage, his friend tried to calm him down. This resulted in him punching a mirror in our bedroom, and he came out covered in blood. I felt my only option was to drive him to A&E. It felt like the longest night of my life. Was this really the end for me and my Prince Charming? We both shouted and screamed at each other once at the hospital. We had become that couple, with various people looking on at the demise of our relationship. I finally drove us home after I was instructed to bring him back the following day when he was sober so they could operate on his hand.

As I lay in bed in the early hours of this New Year's Day, I finally felt numb. I was lying next to a man I now saw no future with, and it broke my heart. I had to tell him to move out. This was, without doubt, one of the hardest decisions I've ever had to make. The love I had for this man was more than I had ever felt for anyone previously, and I doubted I'd ever feel this way again.

The events that followed did not surprise me, only confirmed my decision that this relationship was over. He had gone to stay with a friend, and I suggested he went to see our dog whilst I was working. I still found it too hard to be around him; knowing you can't be with someone you love was too hard for me to face at this point. He took our dog, I presume this was in the hope I would take them both back. It is still astounding to me that I was able to let go of her, but I knew that I was doing this for all of us. We could not continue as we had been, and I could not put her through any more of our volatile relationship.

The blame, however, cannot fall on only him. There were two people in that relationship. What I've come to realise is the more you allow someone to behave in a certain way, the more they will. I didn't voice my opinions, and I didn't truly say how I was feeling. This only led me to act out, searching for someone else to validate me. Although I never did cross this line entirely, I wanted to, and I'd laid the groundwork for a back-up. I didn't know how to be on my own and didn't think I was a proper woman without a man there to validate me.

Some people might wish a relationship never happened or regret it going on for as long as it did. I've just learned to appreciate the lessons and the love that I felt. Going forward, you can only wish for people to be happy, and thankfully I'm now at a stage where I actually mean that to be true for him.

Weekend offender

Now I'm pretty sure most women will have had this type of guy in their lives; if not, you've had a lucky escape! He's easy on the eye, a gym type – in this case, my PT. I know, so cliché, but I don't have a receptionist, so he was the next best thing. He started as a concerned friend. I frequently went to the gym, and there he was. As I previously said, I haven't got much of a filter, so when asked how I am, I'm usually honest. So, he was there for me while I was going through what turned out to be the end of a relationship. Gave me a cheeky wink and tried to make me smile.

Fast forward to the end of said relationship. One of my most used mottos in life is, 'To get over, you've got to get under' – under someone else, that is, and fast. Maybe not my wisest motto, but one that I and most of my girlfriends have lived by. In this case, I knew by doing this, I could never go back to my previous relationship.

The two of us had a conversation about how we could be friends with benefits. I was not naive to his fuckboy attitude. He would tell me about some of his conquests, although I tried to explain to him that telling me this didn't make him sound attractive. But in a man's world, when you've lost count of how many women you've slept with, it makes you something of a legend.

So, I find myself in his house, having had an average experience, to put it bluntly. When you have to explain to a man that they haven't actually made you orgasm, it doesn't help the mood. He's the type that really does believe he's God's gift to women; he even told me once that even his exes that hate him always come back for more. All this does is confirm the fact that not enough women are having their needs met properly if this is the sort of thing they go back for.

So, I'm in his bathroom freshening up, butt naked, when his phone starts to ring. He shouts to me to keep quiet, so I presume it's his mum or something and doesn't want the complicated questions. 'Baby girl', I hear him saying. He's definitely not talking to his mum. I really don't think anyone can get away with saying that past the age of 15, or if you're saying it in some sort of rap song. The conversation continues with him trying to convince whoever is on the other end of the phone that he is alone and, of course, no one else is there. When he finally finishes on the phone to this poor girl, all he can muster saying to me is, 'I guess you want to go.' Without saying a word, I try to cling on to what dignity I have left and quickly dress and get as far away from him as possible.

End of chapter? Not quite. The problem is with characters like these, they lie for a living. Having got home after shouting and pounding the dashboard of my car, I receive a long message trying to say, 'It's not what it seems. She's crazy, she's an ex, it's easier if I just go along with it, or she'll get upset.' How many times do we women have to be called crazy before a man is actually held accountable for his actions!?

Unfortunately for me, at the time, I was in a pretty vulnerable state. After a few days and, let's face it, a few awkward encounters at the gym, I chose to believe his sob story. I can't actually fit into one chapter how many times I was duped by this guy after this – frankly, it's too embarrassing to admit. The utter bullshit that came out of his mouth was worthy of an Oscar. But me being me, I continued to try to stay friends with him after all that went on.

He will still text me every couple of months, try his luck, say I will always be the one that got away. Frankly, I think I'm the only one that called him out on his own bullshit. No one can surely have such a high opinion of themselves otherwise. The thing is, with me, a lot of the time, it's not even that much about the sex – it's about the emotions. And when it's like a rollercoaster, I seem to want to stay strapped in.

So, what did happen to the girl on the phone? At the beginning of this sordid mess, he kept saying he was going to properly finish things with her for me. It never even occurred to him that I might not actually want him. A pregnancy (hers, not mine) got in the way of this, although no baby has ever appeared, and I'm not totally convinced there ever was one. To my knowledge, they are still very much together, without child.

Oh, and 'Weekend Offender'? Yes, that is very much printed on one of his skin-tight t-shirts.

Advice from my father

Now my dad is probably the last person I would ever go to when it comes to dating or relationship advice. Not that he has no experience – we've just not really had that sort of open relationship.

My dad is as Catholic as they come; priests and nuns used to be invited to his birthday parties. I even once said I wanted to be a nun in the hope I'd become the favourite child. As you can probably tell by my book, that career path didn't work out.

I stopped living with my dad when I was still very young, so he never really had to experience his four daughters' teenage years. He only saw what we allowed him to see every other weekend. I remember one time my sister hiding her boyfriend under her bed when my dad turned up to see us. As far as he knew, we were all like the Virgin Mary. At some point, this belief was crushed, but I think that was probably done by my eldest sister.

I was 17 when I shattered his dreams. I'd moved out with my boyfriend, just down the road from my mum, so close enough that I could run back when I didn't want to make dinner for myself. We both thought it best to keep my dad in the dark about his youngest daughter moving in with her boyfriend. Unfortunately, not everyone felt the same, and my eldest sister decided to tell him what was really going on.

As you can imagine, it did not go down well. If he'd had a

chastity belt, I'm pretty sure he would have fixed it on me in that moment. His wannabe nun was definitely not going to work for God. He slowly softened as the years went on, but it was six years before my long-term boyfriend and I were allowed to sleep in twin beds in the same room, even though we had been living together for four years at this point.

It comes as no surprise that he was not my first point of call for relationship advice. Nonetheless, the advice came. It felt like only a matter of weeks after my break-up that my father started offering up advice. I think he feels that without a man in my life to look after me, I would no doubt be an eternal spinster, or worse, a lesbian. We're pretty sure he suspected my sister was one, as she kept her relationships under lock and key, and he was overjoyed when she finally introduced him to a boyfriend in her late twenties. It never occurred to him that, more often than not, I did most of the looking after, and that the men in my life were more of a hindrance than a help.

His first attempt at support and advice took me somewhat by surprise. I think both of us felt mutually awkward about the conversation. It was similar to the time I had to ask him if I could get some Tampax, which was greeted by muffled tones and grunting, trying to avoid the conversation as much as possible. Just to remind you, the current year was 2018. He started trying to ask if I was looking for a new suitor. His advice to me at this point was to join an evening class, as I may meet someone there. Thankfully he didn't go quite as far as to persuade me to go to church.

Most recently, when I went to his house, again, my relationship status became something of a discussion topic. I tried to reassure him that I was, in fact, quite happy on my own. He, of course, did not give up. He told me about a horse-riding holiday for singles in Ireland that *The Telegraph* proclaims is very successful. At this point, I had to remind him that I had, in fact, never been a fan of either horse riding or horses, for that matter, in favour of small cuddly animals and that I probably wouldn't have much in common with the people that did. My vision of the sort of people that might go on these holidays, plus the fact I was having this conversation with my father, made any libido I had disappear instantly.

He did not give up there, however! No, let's make this conversation a bit more awkward. He asked if I'd mind if my stepmother joined in on the conversation, and out of pure compliance with him, I agreed. Thankfully my stepmother had my back and reminded my father that women are able to survive on their own, as she did for many years previous to him.

I've decided his next idea will be me learning how to become a shepherd or drive a combine harvester as he seems to have taken to living in the Somerset countryside and would no doubt like me to move closer to keep an eye on me.

Camino

If someone had told me when I was first getting clean at eighteen that I would take up walking for fun, I would have probably run back to the squat I had been living in as quickly as possible. Growing up, both my parents encouraged us to be out in nature, and our weekends would be spent collecting kindling wood for the fire or picking blackcurrants to make a crumble. It sounds idyllic to me now, but at the time, it was a right pain in my arse. I'm sure when I was very small, I may have enjoyed it, but I seem to only remember being put out by it now. It was too cold, my legs hurt, and why couldn't we sit in front of the tv like other kids did? I look back at it now and realise my parents really did try to enrich our lives growing up, but I just wanted to fit in, and all the other kids at school didn't do this.

Last year for my sister's thirtieth, after watching *The Way*, she decided she wanted to walk the last 120 km of the Camino de Santiago. At this time, my relationship with Prince Charming only appeared to be deteriorating, and I felt that I, too, could do with getting away, even if it did mean walking miles. I often agree to things without fully understanding the enormity of what I've signed up for. My own father walked this pilgrimage in his late teens, way before it became the tourist attraction it is today. He and his friend carried tents and various other equipment to complete this walk, with some monks taking pity on them one night and offering them a warm bath and bed to sleep in. Up until this point, I had never really done the traditional backpacker's holiday; I spent my supposed 'gap year' detoxing from heroin in rehab and trying my best not to die.

So, here I was with all the gear – well, nearly – and no fucking idea. What I realised in this week of walking is how much determination I had that, to be honest, I didn't know existed. I fell back in love with walking and nature, as if I was a little girl again, pre-angry-teenage-angst. I couldn't believe how therapeutic it was to strip myself bare and just walk. It was safe to say I caught the walking bug. Fast forward to my relationship ending, and having lost all hope and zest for life, I decided it was time for a walk.

I had never been away alone, I had never travelled alone – I had never needed to. I always had a boyfriend or sister or parent to accompany me. But I was single now, and although I could have asked someone to come with me, something inside me told me I needed to do this alone. I had no confidence in myself or my ability to not only travel but to even book a holiday. Someone had always helped me, and the one time I had tried to book accommodation for me and my sister in Ibiza, I ended up booking us a tent on a weird hippie commune where they swam naked and grew and smoked loads of weed. It was safe to say she was more than happy to help me book this trip.

Most people who do the Camino do it the traditional way and turn up at various hostels in hope they have a spare bed. I was feeling brave, but not this brave. I decided to book each hostel I planned to stay at, so I at least had that as a safety net. I decided to go back and start from the beginning in a place called St Jean Pied de Port. This was a new journey I was on, and I really did feel like I was at the beginning all over again. I arrived in Biarritz terrified and completely out of my depth. The only French I knew was the lyrics from 'Lady Marmalade', and right now, 'Voulez-vous coucher avec moi, ce soir?' wasn't going to help me.

Thankfully I had organised a transfer from the airport to the starting village. The minibus was full of other pilgrims about to start this journey of supposed enlightenment. I realised very quickly how shy I was; I felt so alone and almost paralysed from talking. The first night, I lay in bed and wanted to cry. I received a message from Prince Charming saying he had heard what I was doing and wished me luck. I felt broken. Most people, when they're trying to get over someone, just sleep with someone else – I am most people. Obviously, that hadn't worked for me, so instead, I decided to fly to a country where I don't speak the language and walk for five days solid, with all my belongings on my back ON MY FUCKING OWN! Insanity.

But this week turned out to be the kindest, most loving thing I've ever done for myself. There were moments of despair, but there were also moments filled with such joy and laughter. I strongly believe that you meet the people you are meant to in life, and on this trip, I definitely did. I met a girl who, like me, was travelling alone and had also come out of a volatile relationship. I'm sure she will never know quite how much she did for me this week as she held my hand whilst I tried to mend my broken heart. I had taken a picture of me and my dog that I wanted to leave somewhere on the walk. I had written a note on the back telling her I would always love her, and Daddy would look after her now. I found the spot on the last day; it was beautiful and had the most spectacular views. I sat and wept for what felt like an eternity, trying to say goodbye to a soul I had spent the last eight years with. Yes, she was a dog, but she was so much more than that. She comforted me in a way that no human ever could, and it broke my heart to have to let go of her.

We arrived in Estella, where I would have to say goodbye to the many pilgrims who had brought a smile to my face on this walk. As they left me to continue on their journey, I decided my walking wasn't quite done. I had seen a cross on the top of a hill and knew I wanted to go there to say goodbye to my Prince Charming. As in many things I have tried to do in my life, it wasn't so straightforward. It didn't have the comforting arrows of the Camino showing me the way, and I appeared to get lost on more than one occasion. I finally reached the top where this cross stood with the view of Estella behind it. I sat and tried to say my goodbye, leaving a piece of jewellery he had given me as some sort of offering to the gods to help me.

I don't think that any walk will ever allow me to let go of her or Prince Charming completely, but finally, I felt like I was on some sort of path to mending the shattered heart I had been left with.

ESTELLA, SPAIN 2018

Camino De Santiago

Sometimes you need to walk 100miles to
begin to mend a broken heart.

The joys of internet dating

Having spent most of my twenties in a relationship, the thought of internet dating was completely alien to me. It is the way you now do things, and everyone else seemed to be pros. I set up a few profiles, but the whole experience made me cringe. This way of self-promoting was not where I felt comfortable. One of my close friends insisted she vetted every conversation I had, although I'm not sure she realised what a full-time job it would be, teaching me how to internet-date successfully. I am what I would call a mongrel – apparently, this is not an attractive way to describe oneself. My dad has Dutch, Jewish and English blood, whereas my mum has English and some Italian. If I were a dog, I would surely be described like this.

Having quite a foreign-sounding name, I was asked by one guy if I was Spanish. I was more than a little confused, having forgotten that he, of course, had not heard my frightfully English accent. Thankfully I realised this before being able to respond. To my friend's horror, however, I did say, 'No, but I am a bit of a mongrel.' I was told by her to fight everything in my being and just try not to be myself – 'mongrel' doesn't sound sexy.

My mongrel joke, however, did continue, and I continued to describe myself as such. Although, like most women, I have numerous hang-ups about my appearance, height, intellect and all-round views of myself as a human being, my humour is not something that I am willing to back down on. I didn't want a bloke that cared if I sounded sexy. I am me, and if they didn't like it, well, to put it frankly, they can fuck off.

Having spent so much of my life hiding behind makeup, push-up bras and figure-solving solutions, although I don't always like it, I am me. I think people forget that when I don't have makeup on, that is actually my face. Yes, it might not be perfectly contoured and have more than a couple of blemishes, but it is still my face.

Being in many long-term relationships, I think you become more comfortable in your own skin. It becomes impossible for your partner not to see you at your worst, yet he still loves you. This is one of the blessings I think comes from being in relationships. Although at the end of my longest relationship, I think the only way to describe my style was 'homeless chic'. 'Chic' probably being a bit generous.

I would often wear my boyfriend's clothes, baggy t-shirts, leggings and Dr Martens. My hair would be in a topknot, and my face would be makeup-free. When I first became single, I realised that I needed to adapt to my new life; wearing my now ex-boyfriend's clothes was no longer acceptable.

The problem with online dating is you only see what they want you to see. How can you tell by someone's picture what their intentions were? I nearly messaged a few people purely to give them some tips on what message they were giving off. I would constantly screenshot pictures and send them to my married friends, urging them never to get divorced.

My basic rule was if they have a selfie in the gym or a half-naked shot, it was a 'no' from me. Some people openly said in their bios that they were purely looking for sex. One guy I remember actually admitted to being married and would only send a picture of what he looked like if you started the conversation. My expectations of the male human race were somewhat dwindling at this point. In pure desperation, I would swipe for men I didn't find attractive but had at least remembered to tidy their room behind them in the photo.

Oh, and then, of course, the fact I don't drink left men completely baffled. When asked if I wanted to meet them for a drink, and I explained I no longer drank, so how about a coffee, I was greeted with mixed responses. Some just didn't respond, some couldn't understand how I managed to live a life without it revolving around alcohol, and then a few thought it was admirable.

This, of course, poses another issue. When speaking to my girlfriends, I often have asked the question, 'Have you ever slept with someone for the first time sober?' More often than not, the answer is a resounding no. In this day and age, we have all come to rely on being drunk to have the confidence to get naked with someone for the first time. The first time I did it sober, I cried. Strangely that relationship didn't work out.

I've now thankfully grown to have confidence without the need for alcohol, but it's preferable that the man is also sober. Something they aren't always happy about. In my experience, though, sleeping with a drunk person when you're sober is like sleeping with a pubescent boy. He thinks he's rocking your world when in fact, he's having sex with the cushion you're sitting on.

I still believe that meeting people authentically is always better, but with this new age of dating, people are reluctant to ask you out in public for fear of being knocked back and would rather check if you're on Tinder first.

Still, this mongrel will continue to be unapologetically authentic.

Mr Attenborough

Now we have your typical boy next door. We met online, as I had decided to spread my dating web a bit further. To some, having a two-to-three-hour drive to get to someone may seem a little far, but I'm under the impression that if you limit yourself to what's on your doorstep, you're not always left with a lot of choice.

We were constantly sending each other voice notes. He turned out to have a great David Attenborough impression, so I was constantly getting him to say stuff in his accent. We just got on and would talk about everything and seemed to have a laugh. We decided to meet halfway on our first date, which I decided was Camberley. I seemed to remember one of my parents' friends living there when I was little, and remember it being quite picturesque.

He had not been put off by me being teetotal and was one of the few that actually admired me for it. As it turned out, his mum was actually a recovering alcoholic, so we had some common ground. We got on really well, and by the end of the date were holding hands and even had a cheeky kiss. I decided to go and stay with him the following weekend in London, as I was going there anyway to see my sister, so what the hell.

We went out for dinner and then back to his. Not being on my doorstep, I feel you can get away with having sex with someone sooner – if two people are happy to do it, why is there always so much judgement on women? When you're in a foreign land, such as London, people don't know you. Having lived in a city for a decade now where people seem to hear if you've farted, going to a city where you're anonymous again feels like you can literally be anyone. You can be that alter ego you've always been too afraid to be, and no one will ever know what you've been up to! It feels liberating to sleep with someone and not feel judged in any way. Only you can judge yourself, and right now, I was living my very overdue footloose and fancy-free years!

The following morning I rang my sister to arrange to meet her. To my shock, she was staying by the next tube stop, having also been on a date. This wasn't technically London, but Surrey, not like the one you see in The Holiday, however.

I met my sister, and as I'm sure so many of us do, we began to plan our Christmases in Surrey with our imaginary broods. We've always wanted to live closer to each other, and maybe the stars were finally aligning.

The following weekend he was meant to come to me, but he had forgotten about a family party. Now at this point, I'm sure most people would just decide to postpone, but in this case, I'm not most people. He told me how his uncle was minted, and it was a Bollywood-themed party. There'd be fair rides, Indian food, and it would be a crack. What better way to get to know someone than to meet their whole extended family? Plus, I'm a sucker for Indian food!

So, the following weekend he picked me up from Clapham, and we drove to West Sussex together. He'd booked a hotel that he kindly paid for. I'd packed the only things I could find that might just get away with being Bollywood themed. The hotel was, well, very average, but it was the closest one to the party. It was right next to Gatwick, so was often used by people just before they went on holiday. The room itself had no proper windows and only a skylight.

We arrived at the party where, of course, his family were keen to meet me. We decided to keep the fact we'd only met twice before under wraps, except from his mum and brother. His mum was lovely and was under the impression that I was perfect and had been sent to him by some higher power. His brother was, well, really hot. I'm ashamed to say I couldn't take my eyes off him. He did, however, have a girlfriend and two children, who also happened to be at the party.

The party was fun; his soon-to-be sister-in-law took a picture of us, drew a heart around it, and sent it to him. Nothing like a bit of pressure to make you want to run in the opposite direction. I seem to do this, though, jump in the deep end only to feel like I'm drowning. After he dropped me back at the station, I realised the feelings just weren't there. I didn't realise how stressful it was having to 'break something off', especially when it's just because you're not feeling it.

I decided to do this really weird thing and just be honest. Well, minus telling him I actually fancied his brother! I told him I just wasn't feeling it. The thing is, we constantly try and fart-arse around telling someone the truth, and more often than not, we end up leading them on because we can't just say we're not that into them. At least if we're honest, we don't need to drag these situations on longer than necessary, even if it feels like you're the worst person in the world when you send that defining text.

All credit to him – he took it like a man and was neither bitter nor rude. This, I have to say, gave me a bit more faith in the male human race, even if it didn't last that long.

I'm a woman and I love sex

So, for as long as I can remember, it seemed to me that the reason we all had sex was to please the man. Obviously, the birth of a child is only possible if a man reaches orgasm, but where do women come into this?

Growing up, sole attention was generally only given to a woman by way of fingering, and for some reason going down on a woman was almost frowned upon and rarely admitted by those who dared to do such a heinous act.

It's always been accepted that men masturbate and watch porn because, well, they're men. I'd like to confirm that I am neither a proclaimed feminist nor a man-hater, only someone who feels women often feel obliged to pleasure a man with little consideration for themselves.

It is still an unspoken rule that men are indeed allowed to poke as many pies as possible and be called a hero, yet if women were to do the same, they would be called every name under the sun.

I have met many of these men along my travels, who are not only hypocritical but selfish. On the other hand, I have met some that almost prefer giving pleasure to receiving it – these are my kind of men. Surprisingly when this is the case, I'm more than happy to do my fair share.

Thankfully the scales have started to move, and there are men that are in tune with your body and can even find that all-important g-spot. To me, these men like and respect your body and you as a person.

I feel there is a stigma attached to women being sexually confident. I've often been called sexually intimidating, which I'm never really sure how to take. Am I, in fact, too full-on and scary? Or is it simply that they're used to women being there only to serve them? I'm not sure which answer is worse.

It still astounds me how different everyone is, the fetishes, the things that really get them going – it is never a one-size-fits-all situation. This is why I think it's important to at least like the person, for you both to get to know each other's likes and dislikes and not be afraid to talk about it.

However, whatever your desires are, I think it's crucial that you're both on board. I will never understand why I'm so often made to feel bad or pressured into doing something I don't want to do, and it seems to be just male banter.

I was lucky enough to have friends that talked openly about sex and masturbating and opened me up to this world before it was too late. This still didn't happen until I was about twenty, so there were a few lost years.

I still speak to women now that haven't ever had an orgasm. This, to me, feels like a crime against the female race. When you know how to make yourself orgasm and get to know your body, I think this really helps. It is the most amazing thing to understand how your body works on a deeper level. Some men do this numerous times a day, so it's about time we got in on the action.

Perhaps no man will ever read this book, but there are a few things I feel, as women, we need to help them understand. A fanny fart is not an orgasm, just because you're wet does not mean you've cum, and just because you've enjoyed it doesn't mean you're finished.

How would men like it if they were about to cum and we stopped?

So, I will continue to speak to my girlfriends and help them feel empowered in their bodies and help them feel confident in asking to get their needs met.

This is not a feminist movement but just a basic human right.

Is chivalry a thing of the past?

Sometimes I wish I was born in a different era. I think that when women were destined to stay at home and simply cook and breed, it was a simpler time. There were definite roles in relationships – men would go out to work and provide while women did, well, absolutely everything else. You worked at a marriage or simply stuck with it because divorce wasn't an option.

I'm not, however, saying this is right, but surely there was less to argue about? I'm what they now would call a modern-day woman; I work full time, am able to support myself financially, sort all household bills out and even fix the occasional pipe. This is because I've had to learn to survive on my own. I don't claim to be like Joan of Arc, and there are close friends I have on standby to help fix things when I have given up using YouTube videos.

In my mid-twenties, I was lucky enough to buy my first property. This would not have been possible without the financial support of my parents. In this day and age, I think it's impossible without it, especially if you're like me and use PayPal all too often to send yourself presents in the post. But I have to say that however lucky I feel to be on the property ladder, more often than not, I've felt men feel emasculated by this.

I've never been attracted to men who have money or are good with money. They all seem to live in the moment and see paying bills or just being an adult as something of an inconvenience. So more often than not, I tend to be the one that earns the most. This begins with them having their ego dented, but over time has led them to take advantage of my good nature.

I would pay for holidays and meals and lend them tenners here and there, all with the promise of being paid back. I even remember agreeing to give an ex money before we went to the pub, so it looked to his friends like he was treating me. I've taken credit out for them to buy the latest laptop they needed for work, only to be left with the repayments when we broke up. I appreciate that the more you give, the more people will take, and it's something I definitely need to work on.

There still seems to be this rule, though, that women are expected to do all the 'pink jobs' – cleaning, cooking, laundry, the list seems endless, even when they've had a ten-hour day standing on their feet. If men remember to do their 'blue jobs' – putting the bins out, fixing a broken pipe or hanging up a picture – we should lay out a red carpet and give them endless blow jobs to say, 'Thank you'.

So, my quest for the modern-day man continues. One that isn't intimidated by my success and doesn't want to take advantage of it either. One that is an equal. This all being said, surely it's still OK to expect the occasional romantic gesture? A bunch of flowers just because, or even a Valentine's Day card.

In previous relationships, I've been convinced that Valentine's Day is nothing but commercial bullshit. I chose to go along with this and say this was also my belief because I knew I would never get anything. But is it really that much against your morals to make your girlfriend or wife feel special? Social media has taken over, and on this romantic day, your feed is filled with women thanking their amazing boyfriends and husbands for the large bouquet of flowers and reminding you how thoughtful they are. This new age of comparison only leads you to yet again feel robbed of something.

Is it possible to have an equal partnership but still be treated like a lady? Will I soon have to buy them flowers and write romantic poems in cards for them to remind them that I love them?

Was chivalry actually created because men were massive arseholes, and by doing these small gestures, they were somehow making up for that? Has feminism gone too far that we can no longer expect the same kindness?

Here's to finding a relationship that is a partnership and not an expectation.

Soulmate

For years I had a crush on this guy; he worked in a shop close to where I lived. He was everything in a man I found attractive, tall, dark and handsome and tattooed. Whenever I saw him, we would share this eye contact that made me feel like he could look into my soul. We had never had long conversations, but I just felt that we shared something. Songs would remind me of him, and I can't explain why, but I just felt I knew him.

Finally, the stars seemed to align, and we were both single at the same time. After slipping into his DMs, we decided to meet up. The first time he came round, we stayed up until 5 am talking, only to have to wake up a couple of hours later to go to work. This was different, it felt different. We didn't even kiss that first night; I think it was about a week later that we met up in the middle of the night just so we could kiss each other. He was like me in so many ways, and he had a deep heart full of scars. He even confessed that he, too, had felt like I could see into his soul, and there were songs that reminded him of me.

I wasn't used to such a sensitive man. He wrote me poems, made pieces of art and would even serenade me with the song, 'I Can't Help Falling in Love with You' after only a couple of weeks. This felt like that drugged-up love, and I was well and truly hooked. A poem I received one morning seemed to send me deeper into this addiction.

Rise and shine, good morning, my soulmate,
It's been a long time coming but it's been worth the wait!

In fact, I've been waiting for rather a long time,
Fantasising about the day I could finally call you mine!

Well, that wait has come to an end, and therefore it seems,
That the universe is ready for me to be with the girl of my dreams!

Therefore, I shall grab this chance and never let it go,
I shall hold it tightly to my chest because now I know...

That I couldn't possibly live without you, and life will never be the same again,
As thanks to you, all I can feel is happiness coursing through my every vein!

So, in return for making me so happy, I promise and I vow,
That nothing will ever harm you as you're with me now!

I shall support you forever and always have your back,
If you ever fall down, I'll be the first to help you up and get you back on track!

Until my dying day, I'll always gaze at how beautiful you look,
And I'd say this to you with the last breath I took....

'Mariella, you're my one and I always knew....
That you'd have my heart and I'd be in love with you.'

With all drugs, there are ups and downs. One minute we'd be high as a kite only to fall down to earth with a bang. He had issues, though, of course, but he was so kind and loving to me and accepted mine, it felt like they just bonded us together more because we understood each other's pain.

One night he ended up in hospital. He'd drunk too much and taken too many drugs. He'd cut his legs to pieces to try to get rid of some of the pain he was feeling. The following day I bathed him; the bath water was a deep red, filled with his blood. Now to many normal people, they probably would have run a mile, but I felt his pain, and I guess, looking back, I wanted to make him better.

Having had my own troubles myself, I tend to empathise with those going through their struggles too. I know that I managed to move on from mine so I always tend to think they could too. One night I couldn't get hold of him; I'd heard nothing from him all day and panic set in. In the end, I rang his mum out of fear he may have really hurt himself this time. Thankfully he hadn't, but he had managed to get himself arrested.

It was no doubt a cry for help or some sort of psychosis. He had rung the police to say there was a man threatening him with a knife. When the police arrived, all they found was a broken man in the street. It was him. He had a knife but, as it turns out, just wanted to be arrested and not do anyone any harm. His mother was called, and she made the six-hour round trip and took him back home to where he had grown up.

For months I didn't hear from him, only making contact with him through his mum or his best friend. I was broken; withdrawal from him was worse than any detox I'd ever encountered. I waited and waited for the day to speak to him and went through many days when he had promised to contact me, only to be left disappointed.

Finally, that day did come. It was like he had never gone, and our love only felt stronger. He was trying to get better, for himself and for us. I drove to him, and my addiction to him started all over again. There was never an awkward silence with us. We would send each other songs that reminded us of one another and positive quotes to get us through our days. Every time I left him to go home, we would both sob.

After a few months of him supposedly not drinking, he took a new job in a new town to start afresh. Our plan was that I would move there, we'd get married and start a family. However, things slowly started to change. He became more distant, and lies would creep in. I think the problem with people is that they think because I don't do drugs anymore, that I've forgotten what the warning signs are. They forget that I'm not a nun.

For a long while, I lied to myself, though. I brushed past the obvious warning signs and believed his web of lies. One thing that addicts become extremely good at is manipulating people so they are able to carry on with their lies that, in turn, are slowly destroying them. I had so many people around me that could see it clearly, but like with any addiction, I chose to ignore all the bad it was doing me and just chased the highs.

I had started the process of buying a house in this new town that was meant to be our fresh start. My offer had been accepted, and we began planning our future together. We were going to start fresh and move on from all the pain and hurt we'd come from.

It was my birthday weekend, one that I've been sure for years has been cursed. We arranged to do lots of fun stuff, and my sister was coming from London to join us. He was never a good sleeper, so I made excuses when he didn't get out of bed until 3 pm and brushed off the fact his first drink was a beer. That night, he let me and my sister sleep in the bed and said he would take the sofa. I went to brush my teeth and found a blue pill on the floor; it was Valium. I confronted him about it, but again he fed me a story that it must have been someone else's. I chose to believe him. The following day we were due to go to a market in town, but when I tried to wake him, he was dead to the world.

I couldn't believe the lies I was telling myself any longer and decided to go through his things. I found hundreds of baggies, only the amount a drug dealer would have, with traces of white powder. I also found about fifty Valium pills tucked away. My earth was shattered. It is impossible to help someone when they aren't ready to help themselves. When he finally woke up, he again promised me the world, made excuses for all the paraphernalia, and swore to me he would change.

My sister left, concerned that this relationship would no doubt drag me back to the place I'd fought so hard to escape from. The following day I woke to find I was alone in bed and suspected he had never actually joined me. All his stuff was still here, but my car had gone from the driveway, and I had no way of contacting him as he had broken his phone. The previous evening he had expressed suicidal thoughts, and I'd begun to panic.

I rang everyone he knew trying to find him, and even rang the police, scared for his welfare, having been convinced by his friend that this was the right thing to do. By this point, everyone was looking for him, and I was putting off having to ring his mum and explain the situation. I couldn't bear to put her through more anguish, but the police were insisting I call her. It got to 8 pm, and I had run out of ideas and excuses why I shouldn't; as I began to dial, he walked through the door.

He was a man I no longer recognised compared to the one that would write me poems expressing that I was his soulmate. I was greeted with anger and rage. Why had I got everyone involved, why had I made such a scene? The following day his friend drove me to where he'd abandoned my car. He had said he'd got two flat tires, but what I was greeted with was very different. The tires were bare, and apart from the fact that there was no obvious denting, you would have thought he'd crashed it.

I had to wait two hours for the RAC to come out, and £300 later, I was on my way home, having had to call in sick to work. I spent most of my drive home hysterically crying, and I think I knew in my heart it was over.

He never pleaded for me to take him back, only pleaded that I left him. Said he would never be good enough for me and that I deserved the world. But around me, my world was broken.

We spoke for a while after and even met up once, but like with many drugs, the highs were no longer in reach. Thankfully I was able to pull out of the house purchase before it was too late. The dream of being that mother and wife had crashed and burned.

He had awoken a part of me I never believed I had wanted. The family, the wedding, the marriage. And so, I was left to pick up the pieces of my broken heart once again, with help from my truly amazing friends.

If I'm honest, this chapter seems a little unfinished. I still struggle with the fact that it's over and understanding why I wasn't good enough for him to want to change. How do you find someone after a heartbreak like this who even comes a little bit close to what you felt?

To many people, I am insane; to myself, I'm insane a lot of the time too. But this felt so real, yet here I am, venturing into the unknown yet again, trying to find someone who understands me like he did.

They say it is better to have loved and lost than never having loved. But why do I keep losing?

Healthy relationship

What is a healthy relationship? The million-dollar question. Am I the only one that doesn't seem to have grasped it? I used to think that it was loving someone in spite of their faults, but maybe they shouldn't have so many to begin with.

I used to scroll the internet for quotes to make sense of the noise that went on in my head, trying to find answers to all my questions. But is this just like watching those rom-coms, giving me a false vision of what my life should be? I've always been extremely stubborn, but not always in my favour. In relationships, I have held on until the bitter end to give them every opportunity when a lot of the time, I should have let them go a long time ago. In my head, I'm thinking, 'I've got to make this work', but what is so bad about just pulling the plug?

All my relationships have ended due to some catastrophic event; it's never been that we've just agreed to part ways. Because of this, I think I wait for the catastrophic event to happen as an excuse to end it, sometimes even having to orchestrate it. I grew up watching series like Friends and rewatching the whole thing time and time again when depression gets the better of me. But it seems in these programmes, break-ups look so simple, apart from Ross and Rachel's 'on a break' situation. They seem to say their piece, no argument, and even a hug and good wishes at the end. I'm yet to work out how to do this.

I think being a people pleaser actually isn't as pleasing as the name makes out, for either person. For me, I'm in constant pain and confusion, trying to separate my own feelings and those of others. While I'm actually being really dishonest to the other person, which more often than not makes them despise me.

I'm definitely known for my overthinking and empathy. I have to go and see my more rational friends on more occasions than their husbands may like for them to simplify things for me and remind me that how I feel matters.

I think most women have pretty vivid imaginations, and even before a date have tested how their name goes with someone's surname and imagines what their children might look like. But this need for marriage and children is still a pretty new thing for me.

I spent most of my twenties condemning the whole sordid affair. I didn't believe in marriage and frankly found children to be something of an irritant. Coming from a broken home, I think you go one of two ways – you either long for that loving family and the security, or you're sworn against it, or so I thought.

It only occurred to me that the reason I was so against the whole idea is that I wasn't with the right person. I wasn't with someone who I saw a stable home with or thought would be a present father. Maybe I just wasn't the one he wanted to be that person with, even if he was unaware of it.

Female hormones have a way of sneaking up on you, though. One minute you're the antichrist with children, the next I find myself holding my friend's baby, sniffing his head and crying. I suddenly realised why some women have 'accidents'. I genuinely felt like I was going insane.

Like when you try to stop smoking, and suddenly everyone around you is puffing away. In the same way, everyone around me appeared to be in families, or pregnant, or getting married, and I was still trying to remind myself to wear a bra on my day off.

Requirements for a new suitor

Now after having, let's face it, some dating disasters, my friend and I decided to make a list of things we did not want in a potential suitor. I think the list probably says more about us than them, but we felt it necessary to make such requirements.

- Not married
- Not gay
- Not homeless
- Not a drunk
- Not alcohol or drug dependant
- Not in a relationship
- Not 'separated' or on 'a break'
- Not broke
- No major mental health problems (that haven't been addressed)
- Has shit together
- Hasn't been to prison
- Has no upcoming criminal charges
- Isn't on tag
- Doesn't live at home in their 40s
- No debt

Now I don't think this is asking too much but believe it or not, I have encountered most of these types of men; they're like a moth to the flame, and I am, unfortunately, that flame. Or maybe I am the moth, and they are, in fact, the flame that wants to burn me alive.

These days I try and look at things more positively than I did when I made this initial man-hating list. One of my sisters encouraged me to look at it a bit differently and not write so much about what I didn't want and more about what I do. Giving positivity out to the universe and all that jazz.

So, this is my revised list...

- Funny
- Finds me funny (definitely important if they end up in my book!)
- Tall
- Self-sufficient
- Has own money
- Kind
- Generous
- Loving
- Helpful
- Creative
- Calm
- Patient
- Cool dude (my sister made me write that)
- Active

- Adventurous
- Social
- Interesting
- Likes animals
- Family orientated
- Makes effort
- Social drinker/non-drinker
- No drugs
- Proportionate and working penis

Now maybe I'm looking for a man that doesn't exist, or that does exist, but I have no chemistry with, but I don't feel like I'm asking for the impossible. My revised list was made whilst soaking up the Ibizan sun, and then the impossible happened – had the universe really been listening?

The Ibizan

Now I don't know about you, but I'm a sucker for an accent; it was not a Spanish one, however. Ibiza is dripping with ex-pats trying to fulfil their dreams, and one just happened to fall in my lap. He was northern, and I always think they somehow sound more manly; he was built like a brick shithouse and had a charm about him. He was a waiter in a bar, and whilst my sister and I sipped on our healthy smoothies, I couldn't help but imagine my life here.

I, of course, made it clear to my sister that I thought he was hot, so she, in turn, shot a million questions at him. He seemed to be ticking all the boxes, it was crazy. He didn't drink, was into fitness and had three dogs – could my dreams be about to come true? My sister was beyond excited, and I had to stop her from searching for a hat for yet another imaginary wedding. The fact he lived here was all the more appealing, as at this point, I was full-on ready to pack up my life in the UK and escape to better climates. To my shock, he wrote his number down on our receipt. I'm more than aware that I don't always come across that well, but again he seemed to be charmed by my awkwardness, or maybe I was more attractive in Ibiza.

But then it dawned on me, was he giving his number to me or my sister? This could become very awkward. I decided to message him, hoping that I hadn't got my wires crossed, and thankfully I hadn't. Now I have to say, I'm usually the first to ditch my friends, or my sister in this case, for the possible love of my life, but something had changed in me. I had come away to spend time with my sister, and it would have to be a pretty mind-blowing proposal for me to leave her.

It was not.

It turns out one requirement was lacking; he was currently living in a tent with his three dogs. You might think this sounds romantic, and had I been offered a candlelit meal or something similar, I probably would have jumped at it. What I was offered wasn't anywhere near good enough to jump ship. He pretty much offered me a booty call, and with no way of leaving his dogs, I was expected to go to his tent. At no point did he mention even having a nice mocktail and was only willing to offer his company. I don't know, but to me, if you only have a tent to offer, and aren't willing to go anywhere yourself, maybe glam it up a bit. Offer to have a BBQ, listen to some music, anything but going to some woods someplace where your tent is.

Although I fancied him and can take care of myself, this is the sort of shit you hear in scary movies, or worse, on the BBC news. I can see the headlines now, 'British girl goes to tent in the Ibizan woods and is tortured and killed.' So no, the universe had not been listening. It would appear it was actually high on drugs and fancied a good laugh. Make this girl think we have answered her prayers, but make him live in a tent!

The Young One

I think after my last catastrophic attempt at a relationship, my friends were more than eager to find someone for me. Someone who was more 'boy next door' than 'boy who can't find the door'. After work one night, I decided to go with some friends to one of our locals. Having had a full day at work and feeling more than dishevelled, my last idea was trying to spot the local talent.

My friends had other ideas. I've always gone for older guys, rarely went for someone my age, and have never gone for anyone younger. Why is it that females going for younger males seem almost predatory, yet men going for younger women is just normal?

Without me realising what was going on, my friends seemed to introduce me to this young man. He smiled shyly at me, then they left us without any warning. For some reason, I didn't want to come across as too rude, so I tried to make some sort of conversation, as this was obviously what my friends wanted. After making pleasantries and being exhausted by the whole thing, I decided to leave. My friend had given him strict instructions not to come on too strong and to just send me a message saying it was lovely to meet me. I didn't really get it, still don't. I appreciate people might find me attractive, but surely there's someone young, dumb and in need of cum that was an easier bet.

I decided to meet him, though – why not? He was sweet and seemed pretty down to earth. He had also been through a not-so-amicable break-up, so we had something in common. In my head, I thought, 'Let's try this whole get under to get over theory again.' He, however, didn't agree. I was going to Ibiza on holiday, and he insisted we wait until I was back. I don't think I've ever put myself on a plate for the taking for someone to turn me down, at least when I knew they wanted it.

He said he didn't want me to get the wrong idea of him, but what idea does that give about me? Although at this point, slightly frustrated, I went along with it.

I was back from Ibiza, and finally, it was time. He did say he found me quite intimidating. This was actually the result of me asking him if he'd ever slept with someone for the first time sober. What 25-year-old male has? This, in turn, made him quite nervous, not that I was aware. We had fun together; I had no expectations of what was going on and didn't really think about it. I think I just thought it was a bit of fun for both of us.

Then came the night it all fell apart. He'd offered to cook me dinner at his. I arrived only to find him quite stressed. That day his ex had dropped off everything he owned in bin bags at his house. We've all been in that relationship. The one we never really wanted to end but ultimately did. Although we can look back with hindsight knowing it wasn't right, at the time, it feels like the walls are caving in. And this was one of those relationships for him.

He seemed a little off, but it was understandable. It's not until you're getting down to it that you realise his whole body had just switched off and wasn't working as we would like. I realised then that it had all got a bit much, and he needed some space. Unfortunately, I hadn't left feeling satisfied, only frustrated. Trying to not take the whole situation personally, I went home to get my reliable battery-operated male equivalent.

But it was just not my night. I lay on my bed, excited by the knowledge that I would soon feel relieved and satisfied. I pressed the on switch, only for it to tell me it, too, was out of juice.

I lay there half laughing, half crying. I appreciate this can be a common thing amongst men, but honestly, it had never happened to me before. Not only did I now feel unattractive to him, but to my vibrator also.

After that, we saw each other a couple of times, but it didn't really take off. Timing is so important, and for him, it wasn't right. My friends did try and apologise for the failed set-up, and I vowed never to let them get involved again. Obviously, that didn't last long.

From this, I can at least take that there was no ill feeling. So many times, it ends badly, only for you to avoid each other at all costs. This wasn't the case for us, and we remained on friendly terms. Still liking each other's social media posts and being genuinely pleased to see each other when we were in social situations.

All is not lost for the male human race!

My throuple

Everyone needs a couple like these two in their life. It's not always easy when one of your closest friends gets married and starts a family, especially when your life seems to be falling apart at the time. Your friendship often goes one of two ways: your bond gets closer, or you try to find more single friends.

I've never been the best at making new friends or relationships, it would seem. I'm a bit like Marmite; you either love me or hate me. It takes some people a while to get through my inappropriate humour and lack of filter.

When I first met my friend, to be honest, I thought she was a bit of a dick, but apparently, that is the beginning of many great friendships. When you're going through hard times in your life, you often realise who your real friends are, and she definitely earned her medals and still continues to do so on a daily basis.

Her husband has embraced me as the official lemon in their relationship, and I'm pleased to say he has become a friend in his own right.

Going out when you've just had a baby is fear-inducing for most sane women and something you'd categorically avoid. But not for this one; her new going-out routine was slightly different, however. Pumping your breast milk and having to wear pads over your nipples so they don't leak isn't everyone's idea of a great start to a night out, but nonetheless, she was not going to give up being my wingwoman.

I've cried on her, her baby, and probably, at times, her husband. They've been like my cheerleaders, being there through every dating and relationship disaster.

Most people look forward to going on their family holidays to get some much-needed time away from their usual working weeks. And most single people probably would rather go to Ibiza to party the night away than be going on someone else's family holiday, but it appears we are not most people.

So yes, I did, in fact, go on a family holiday with these two and their beautiful boy in tow. I'm not going to say I wasn't slightly hesitant; do you really want to be around something you yourself are longing for? In all honesty, this was one of the most fun holidays I'd had. At no point did I ever feel left out or like I was intruding on their first holiday with their baby.

It became a running joke that we were a throuple. I don't think people really knew what the fuck was going on, one waiter even referring to me and my friend as her husband's women. Most sane people would no doubt try and ghost me, find reasons for me to stop coming around and crying to them about my latest disaster, but not these two.

At Christmas, they gave me a key to their house, only confirming that they are, in fact, here to support me regardless of the changes that are happening in their lives. And, as of yet, they haven't changed the locks.

The Friends enthusiast

I was days away from going away with my throuple when I started talking to this guy. With no possibility of seeing him anytime soon, we decided to get to know each other just by messaging.

One thing I've definitely learnt from this experience is that this is not a good idea, not for me anyway. More often than not, I'm living in a fantasy land. I get images in my head of how this person will be, only to be left disappointed upon meeting them.

Also, I usually have an array of friends around me, some telling me not to get too carried away and some getting ready to plan my upcoming nuptials with this unsuspecting man. I was definitely on holiday with the wedding planners.

We had so much in common that it was scary. I was on holiday with my couple friends and their baby, and he lived with his couple friends and their baby. We shared a love for all things *Friends* and would often use their memes throughout our messages. In the evening, I was often back in my room fairly early, so my friends were able to get their baby to bed, so I spent my evenings messaging him, and we both opened up about anything and everything: failed relationships, how they went, etc.

My friends were convinced he was 'the one', promising to do the famous dance Monica and Ross did on *Friends* at our wedding. Strangely he seemed as hooked on the whole idea as me, his friends who he lived with even saying we will either be married in the week, or it would be a disaster. There were some warning signs, I think, but I chose not to look into them too much. In this day and age, sending a photo of yourself that day isn't a big deal, but he seemed reluctant to do it. Also, voice notes or even talking on the phone to someone you've never met becomes pretty normal, yet I pretty much had to force him to speak on the phone to me. But I put this down to him being nervous.

We were due to be back in the UK early Saturday morning, and I was due to meet him on the Sunday, but after a week of nonstop talking, I couldn't wait any longer. He agreed to meet me on the Saturday and although I was exhausted, having not had much sleep, I was buzzing. I got ready and even went round my throuple's house to make sure I looked OK – they clearly hadn't had enough of me.

We had decided to meet in the cathedral grounds and go look inside and then go to a local historic pub. Romantic first date, I thought. He arrived, and almost instantly, I got a bad vibe – had I just expected too much? He just seemed really awkward, not something I'm used to. Everyone I've met has always been quite confident and managed to laugh at the awkward first meeting.

We walked around the cathedral, but I knew he wasn't what I had expected. It didn't feel natural. I was so disappointed, but I knew that I had to give it a chance, so we continued to the pub. He ordered a Guinness, and I ordered a Diet Coke. I took out my wallet, more out of politeness than to pay and was shocked when he didn't protest. Now I'm not high maintenance and probably over-generous if anything, but I do like a man to be a bit of a gentleman, at least. As his drink cost three times what mine did, I would expect him to pay or at least offer.

By this point, my mind was pretty much made up. He

asked me if he was what I expected, and I said no. He also agreed I wasn't what he had expected. It was ridiculous – in my head, I had really thought I was meeting a guy I was going to spend the rest of my life with, and in reality, it was so far from that. At this point, I was exhausted and more than a little upset, and the worst possible thing happened – I started to cry. I mean, have you ever heard of anyone crying on a first date? I was mortified; he was pretty sweet about it, but I made my excuses and we parted ways.

On my walk home, I rang my sister, crying the whole way home, saying how I'm never going to meet anyone. Back to the Ben and Jerry's I went.

The following day my throuple kindly invited me over for a roast so I could give them a step-by-step account of the hideousness that was my date. To my shock, he messaged me wanting to see me again. He explained that he had been nervous and would like to try again. Now I'm not sure if this is just me, but I really don't think you should have to try this early on. Maybe years down the line, but not after a first date. I explained this to him as nicely as I could, only to receive a message from him saying, 'I'm obviously not broken enough for you.' WOW.

Well, if my mind wasn't already made up, that ought to do it! Strangely he almost contradicted himself in that moment. What kind of person says that? Having been open about my past relationships, I never expected it to be used against me. I actually would like someone who's got their shit together and isn't broken, I don't seek them out in hope I'll be able to fix them.

The reason I didn't want to see him again wasn't that he wasn't broken enough; it just didn't feel right, and that is a good enough reason.

Camo shorts

The lesson I learnt most from this individual is not to judge someone by what they wear at work. If you're like me, any tradesman has a certain appeal. They all look a bit rough round the edges and give off that rugged look. Unfortunately, they don't always have the same charm.

This was another friends' set-up. I was passed his number and thought, 'What the hell!', bored and lonely and still trying to find my mate. After exchanging a few messages, we decided to go on a date. He always seemed really attractive to me: a bit bohemian, long hair and liked to travel. I spent a fair bit of time making sure I had the right outfit and decided to team it with some flip-flops so as not to come off like I was trying too hard. For a change, I felt like I looked pretty good and was excited for what the night may bring.

As per usual, I was a bit early, so I tried doing a loop of the block to stop myself looking too eager. I saw him approaching and had butterflies in my stomach – maybe this was it. Those butterflies soon flew off. He appeared in camo shorts, a black vest and a red checked shirt. On his feet, he wore the sort of trainers I wore when I was about eleven, Gola type, teamed with some sort of trainer socks. It was an outfit I would expect my dad to wear, not my date.

I tried not to judge, but I think I'd have preferred it if he'd turned up in his work clothes. We got shown to our table, and he was dripping with sweat. I appreciate it was a hot day, but when someone then has to wipe their brow with the napkin provided for your meal, it's not exactly a turn-on. He was about six years older than me but hadn't aged well. His skin looked weathered and in need of some deep moisturiser. But I tried to look past the outfit and the sweat dripping from him and see if we actually had anything in common.

Before the date, we'd already arranged to spend the following day together going to the beach. I knew pretty soon that there was no romantic chemistry, and this was purely a friend-zone situation. Unfortunately, I'm not very good at expressing myself and didn't have the heart to say I didn't want to spend the following day together. In all honesty, I had no other plans, and all my friends were tied up with their families. Who doesn't like the beach, after all?

The following day we drove a couple of hours to Lulworth Cove, a beauty spot, but often full of tourists. As we drove, we seemed to be driving away from the sun. I, of course, was dressed for the summer, as it was due to be nearing thirty degrees that day. On arrival, this particular beauty spot was hidden by cloud and fog. I was a typical Brit wearing next to nothing, and with no hope of this man keeping me warm in any way, we decided to find a nearby restaurant. They were all packed with hopeful Brits, scantily clad, who also appeared to be in search of the sunshine we all had driven away from.

Thankfully for my job, I have learnt the skill to talk to almost anybody, and we did share a love for travelling, even if this was the only thing we shared. We decided to have a bite to eat, and I insisted on paying as he had paid for our meal the previous evening. I'm not into allowing men to pay for me, especially when I know it's not going to go any further.

After my much-needed trip to the gift shop to purchase a souvenir to remember this rather awkward date, we decided to drive home. As we drove, I could see the last fragments of the sunshine that had been engulfing our city. Upset that I had missed out on possible tanning time, I swiftly said my goodbye and tried to get into the last corner of sunshine in my courtyard.

Now, this guy was lovely, just not for me. Not a bad bone in his body, polite and kind, so of course, I had no attraction to him whatsoever. Not long after I got in, I received a message from him. He was so sweet, said how nice it was to spend time together, etc. I hate leading people on, and I think it's better to just rip the Band-Aid off. I replied, saying it was nice spending time together and no doubt I'd see him around. I thought I was being nice but putting up the boundaries. Some of my friends, however, disagreed and thought I'd been a tad harsh.

So thankfully, I thought I didn't have to see him again and encounter any more awkwardness, but this is me, and for some reason, awkward encounters hunt me down. A few hours later I realised I had, of course, left my trainers in his car, thinking at the time that we might go for a walk in the sunshine. This led to me having to contact him to get them back, and he kindly said he'd drop them off. When he arrived, I had to deal with the fact that I didn't want to invite him in, even for a drink. He sort of hovered until I made my excuses and bid him a farewell.

Now maybe it was karma for being blunt, or maybe my life tends to lead me to places where I want to die in that moment. The next time I saw him was in the doctor's surgery. I had gone in to drop off a stool sample, embarrassing enough when you don't even know anyone. But of course, he was standing in front of me in the queue.

He was there booking appointments for inoculations to go travelling, and I was holding my own poo.

If that isn't some sort of fucked-up karma, I don't know what is.

Can you still meet men in bars?

Is there actually any point in going on the prowl on a night out anymore? I can honestly say that when I'm out, it's rare that I ever get chatted up. Whilst in relationships, I perfected my resting bitch face to keep men away from me. I wasn't aware I had even done it until a caring friend gave me the advice that maybe I should smile more.

The days of underage foam parties where you'd joyfully accept some horny teenager grinding up against you while you were slut-dropping were over. I think I almost grew to hate men and any advances they might try to make on me. I remember clearly learning this from my sisters. Some weird feminist action, maybe, or just sick of men assuming they could feel you up whenever they saw fit. One unsuspecting man once slapped my sister's bum, only to get greeted with a punch in the face. So, I guess I was brought up with some fiercely strong women.

I remember clearly being out with two of them in a bar in Brighton, dancing the night away. We were definitely not on the lookout and just wanted to enjoy an evening of dancing to good music. Whenever a bloke even tried to invade our circle, we would stop dancing and just glare at them. This sent off even the strongest of men back to their friends with their tails between their legs. So, this habit kind of just stuck, and I was something of a man-repellent whenever I went out.

Fast forward to my friend's advice for me to smile more, and I have to be honest, I did take it on board. The problem is when you're nice to men, they tend to think they've scored, but that is merely the first building block. My sharp tongue tends to come out and take them down a peg or two, which in turn leads to them giving up because, let's face it, that pissed-up girl in the corner is a much easier target.

So comes the other slight issue with being a non-drinker on a night out. To be clear, I can have as much fun, if not more fun, than most people out. The difference is I no longer hang out with people that aren't fun to be around. If you have to drink to enjoy someone's company, they're probably not your kind of people. I'm able to dance, laugh and joke completely sober because I've taught myself to have the confidence to do that. This and the fact I think everyone else is pissed and either thinks I'm pissed or is too worried looking at themselves to worry about whether I'm a good dancer or not. I stay out until all the clubs shut, sometimes even go to an after-party and sit on the side of the road with my heels off eating cheesy chips covered in ketchup just like the rest of you. I just remember what I've done the next day, and unfortunately for my friends, remember what they've done too.

So, after trying this whole weird smiling thing, I started to attract some people. More often than not, it was people that I frankly wouldn't touch with a barge pole, but at least I was no longer repelling them! Then comes the issue that all men in bars are, well, drunk. Maybe the shit chat works on Sally over there who's had one too many cocktails, but I need a bit more.

Where I live, everyone seems to know everyone, and you always see the same faces in the same bars, time after time. This only leads to me going out once in a blue moon to see if they've improved their chat since last time I saw them. I always had the same guy chat me up, and when I say chat up, I'm being pretty generous. He's typically boyband pretty, and I'm sure has no problems with the ladies, but appearance isn't everything. People become very unattractive when they can't hold a conversation. When he first appeared to be trying to make his move, his conversation was pretty limited, and he thought I'd throw myself in his direction when he loudly told his friend that I wanted to fuck him.

Now having spoken to him on about six previous nights out, you would expect the guy to at least have the courtesy to remember my name. But no, and I point blank refused to talk to him unless he could remember. At the end of the day, if I'm that desirable to you, I think you'd remember my name. He tried and tried every other angle, even trying to say that a guy I was with was going to try and ruin me; this man was actually married with children. Since when has talking about another man fucking your brains out become a chat-up line? Or maybe I'm just old school, but 'you look nice' is still OK.

When I finally decided to go home, he offered to walk me to the taxi rank, by which point someone had finally helped him out and yet again told him my name. He confidently said he was coming back to mine with me. I'm pretty sure if you're not Ryan Gosling in *Crazy Stupid Love*, this isn't going to work. Again, I knocked him back, only for him to reply with, 'Well, we can go to mine.' And that's not even the best bit – he said we didn't need to do anything. How noble! But no means no, and I told him if he was really that bothered to take my number and message me. Funnily enough, I never did receive a message, only a follow on Instagram.

Am I the only one that can't sleep with someone that has

zero chat?

Just because I'm sober doesn't mean I'm boring, it just means I know where my car is, and I'm not hitting on your boyfriend.

The Cypriot

Well, there was one date that came from going out in bars. Because of the nature of where I live, I'd seen this guy around a fair bit. The first time we came into close contact, we were in the gym. I was doing my fitness plan given to me by Weekend Offender, which at times, I felt was orchestrated just to make me look like a twat.

Now I don't know about everyone else, but I definitely don't look like the people that take selfies in the gym. I'd found a quiet room to get on with my hopping and skipping. I'm sweating, out of breath and honestly looking like I've just been dragged through a hedge backwards. It is by far the worst place to bump into someone you fancy, in my opinion. Nothing about what I'm doing is remotely sexy and is only done to make up for the sharing-size bar of chocolate I had instead of dinner last night.

In he comes and starts doing some kung fu moves on the boxing bag listening to heavy metal, a female version of a wet dream. I wanted to run out of the room as quickly as I could for fear of making a complete tit out of myself, but also knowing that, in fact, that would probably make me look worse and, also knowing that Dairy Milk does not burn the calories off for you.

I would always see him around, but it never even occurred to me that he might fancy me, especially after witnessing my moves in the gym. But on one of my rare nights out, he actually approached me. He told me he had always thought I was pretty and could he have my phone number. At this point, I feel he deserves some massive award. He didn't use some cheesy chat-up line, nor did he try and go home with me that night; he actually wanted to take me out on a date.

We arranged to go for dinner. I was pretty concerned that it was actually a set-up and I would be stood up. I remember calling my friend on the phone, chain-smoking cigarettes, and walking laps of the block because, as per usual, I was really early and didn't want to come across as over-keen.

He did turn up, so I guess the joke was on him. He seemed really sweet, wasn't a massive drinker but definitely a bit of a stoner. I've never really had an issue with stoners; I've always preferred them to drinkers, as they're far more predictable. The date actually went pretty well, and he ended up coming back to mine. I had to use all my self-control for it not to go too far because, apparently, putting out doesn't get you love, something I've become far too accustomed to learning.

In the days that followed, we exchanged a few messages, but definitely not the amount I'm used to. He didn't have social media, so I couldn't do any stalking. I always find it a bit suspect when people don't. I wasn't really convinced that he liked me that much, and it definitely wasn't shown through the messages.

We did arrange to meet up again, though, and this time I feel like I was a little less intimidated by his looks. He was really chatty in person, which put me at ease again, but what followed, I couldn't quite get my head round. I am by far not an intellectual or particularly bright, but I like to think I'm not a complete idiot.

He started off by telling me about a trip to Thailand he

had taken. I was pleased because I love travelling and talking about different destinations. He then told me that he had left it too late to get his inoculations for pneumonia and glandular fever. Now, I'm no medic, but I'm pretty sure neither thing is either an inoculation or something you can catch from going to Thailand.

He then went on to tell me his dad was from Cyprus, which to me would suggest he originated from there, so I said, 'Oh, you're half Cypriot.' He responded by saying no, his dad was Scottish, he just lived in Cyprus, but had been back living in Salisbury for at least five years. Now, my dad was born in Angola, but this doesn't make him an African man, nor does it make me mixed raced. I was left a little speechless.

After this, we did carry on messaging for a bit, but I think what really broke it for me was when he described something as 'gangster'. I am by no means a snob and have done my fair share of living in such a way that people would no doubt look down on me for, but when trying to find someone I might like to have children with, I don't think I'd be able to cope with the father saying, 'That's gangster' when our child comes out of my area.

So, it might be time I stopped trying it with these gym types – they may be lovely in some cases, but you just can't have too much of a conversation with them. If they don't message you a lot, it might be a sign.

Hobo Love

Before I start, I'd like to make clear I have nothing against hobos, homeless people or anyone that might fall under that bracket. I myself would have easily passed for one in previous years and, in fact, was close to becoming one.

I do these days mostly pass for an up-together member of society unless you catch me on my day off or visiting my local in my pyjamas in need of a chocolate fix.

I never really noticed the attention I got until a good friend pointed it out to me. As in most towns, there are usually people that hang out in groups, getting away from the hostel they've been faced with living in.

One evening I decided to venture out for an evening of dancing and catching up with my friend. As we walked into town, she noticed that anyone who fitted the description previously stated would find some excuse to talk to me. Whether it was simply asking me for a lighter or catcalling me in some way, shape or form. She told me how she felt invisible to these people, and their attention was purely fixed on me.

I laughed and brushed it off, but after being made aware of this, I've come to notice it more often. On one occasion, I even got asked out when nipping out for a cheeky fag break. The conversation went something like this...

'Oh, you're not from round here.'

'Well, no, I grew up in Reading.'

(Before you judge, just remember Ricky Gervais and Kate Winslet also came from there.)

'Oh, I used to have a mate there who lived in the Salvation Army. You might know him, **man's name*.'*

'Name doesn't ring a bell.'

'Let me take you out for dinner. Imagine the look on people's faces when we walk down the promenade together. You're beautiful.'

'I'm OK, thanks.'

'Oh, but we could walk arm in arm. I've still got a few miles left in me.'

'That's very sweet of you, but I'm going to say no.'

This man was, I'm guessing, in his late fifties, or like many of us, had had a hard paper round. His clothes looked as though he had been wearing them for years, and his hands were dirty – again, not judging, just describing what I see.

Now I have to say I'm partly flattered, partly in shock. I'm not sure where the promenade he speaks of is, and not entirely sure where our dinner plans would have been, but I wasn't in a rush to find out.

Then the other day, I got stopped again. Different guy this time.

'Can I stop you? Don't worry, I'm not going to ask you for anything.'

(A phrase often used, and I have myself used.)

'Yeh course, don't have anything anyway.'

'I just think a compliment isn't a compliment unless it's said out loud, and I'd just like to say you look fucking gorgeous.'

'Oh, well, thanks.'

'Your dress, your hair, your tattoos, you just look mint.'

'Ummm, thanks.'

(Receiving compliments has never been my strong point.)

'Now you have a lovely day.'

'You too.'

These days, I'm going to take any compliments I can, but I do wonder what it is about me that makes these sorts of people approach me. Having been told I have an issue with my resting bitch face, I'm puzzled, to say the least.

I appear never to be approached by anyone else. When out with my friends, it is usually them that get approached while I hover aimlessly in the background. I'm still going to hold onto these occasions and think at least I'm doing it for someone!

Maybe the man of my dreams is, in fact, busking on the corner or begging for a couple of quid in the market square, and I've just not come across him yet. While I'd like to be approached by someone that has at least the use of a shower, I do still take these as compliments, although I'm sure my friends aren't overly jealous of the attention.

They honestly don't know what they're missing!

Rare steak

You would like to think that a man as good-looking as this had the goods to back it up. Imagine the epitome of tall, dark and handsome, the sort you would definitely trip up over or accidentally drive your car into a pole looking at.

He was a friend of a friend, and frankly, I was shocked that I hadn't been introduced to him before. He was the sort of person that any single woman looking for a sperm donor would jump on.

He wasn't my usual type, clean-cut and appeared to know how to use a shower and even an iron. But I wasn't looking for anything too serious and feel you need to experience all types of men before claiming that they're not what you're looking for.

Why is it so difficult to message someone and just simply ask them out? We always feel the need to make up some elaborate story as to why we are messaging them. I always seem to be the one that has to make the first move. I could probably count on one hand the number of times I've actually been asked out. It has previously been explained to me that if we were to wait for a man to approach us, we are simply only giving those men a chance that have 'chosen' us. But in this day and age, if you want something, you have to go for it; that way, you have the choice. Women-power and all that jazz!

As previously explained, conversation starters aren't my strong point, so this was left to one part of my throuple.

She proceeded to message him for me, explaining how I had been told by said throuple to message him. She began by saying I was interested in going travelling and asking him for tips. Obviously, none of this was true. This message was sent, with no essence of me in it at all. Cool, calm and collected, Everything I'm not. So, our plan was in motion! I was about to encounter this dreamy individual, but what I was greeted with was slightly different.

We arranged that we would both go around our friend's house to, of course, talk about my plans to go travelling. Apparently, just asking someone for a night of passion was out of the question. In all honesty, I think this would have been a better idea. Had I not had the following dialogue with him, I may have, in fact, had the night of my life.

I went to my friend's, full of excitement. He wasn't much of a talker and the conversation at times was a bit of a struggle. But alas, I wasn't hoping to marry this guy, so decided to power through. We talked about the best places to go solo travelling and shared stories of where we had both been and would like to go. It wasn't a complete flop, but my fanny wasn't in an immediate flutter.

I had decided to get a yoga swing after going to Ibiza and seeing a video on YouTube of a girl who had far more grace and poise than I did. Obviously, my friends thought this was a great thing to tell this unsuspecting man, so this at least encouraged a bit of flirting. After I left, I felt a little disappointed, but I convinced myself everyone is a bit nervous when they first meet, so maybe we can ramp things up a bit on the chat. At this point, I was done with love and was only looking for a gap filler, no pun intended.

The conversation that deflated any possibility of a summer fling on the swing was about meat. Yes, you read that right. How we got onto the subject of meat, I will never be entirely sure. One minute we were talking about my yoga swing and how flexible I was, then we were talking about steak and kebabs. I like food as much, if not a little more than the next person, but asking me how I like my steak cooked and telling me you like yours with blood oozing out is hardly pillow talk. To not only talk about your love of rare steak but then to start talking about kebabs!? I felt like it was 3 am and we were sitting on the curb outside a nightclub, smashed. It was, in reality, mid-day on a Wednesday, and I just didn't know how I could possibly go from this conversation to some actual pillow talk.

Do we live in a day and age where talking about rare steak is a turn-on? Did I miss something? One of my friends was convinced this was some sort of weird innuendo, one that was honestly lost on me.

However, the two other people in my throuple, whose friend he was, did not agree. The reason they didn't agree was they, too, had had a similar conversation with him about steak and kebabs just the week before.

And so, it seems that no matter how good-looking you are, especially as I was no doubt punching, talking about kebabs and steak will not get you anywhere.

The midlife crisis

Over a matter of about three months, I seemed to become something of a magnet to the older man. Age has never been an overly big issue for me, well, not if they're older, but it seemed weird that it appeared to happen in such quick succession.

The Doctor

When I first relocated and decided to start afresh, I had to find a new doctor, dentist, etc. For me, this is something that fills me with a fair amount of anxiety. I'd been recommended a doctor who was very sympathetic to someone who had had my previous lifestyle; believe it or not, some doctors have not been able to be quite so accepting.

This man was my doctor for eight years, and I'm embarrassed to say I relied on him probably a bit too much, but at no point did he ever make me feel bad for my frequent visits and breakdowns. He once said to me he would rather it was me than an 80-year-old with piles. I would only ever see him, and so he was my go-to for everything, even things many women would prefer discussing with a female doctor. I, however, felt crippling anxiety whenever the receptionist tried to book me in with someone else.

I got a phone call before Christmas one year from him informing me that he was leaving and that I should make an appointment so we could make the transition more comfortable for me. A couple of weeks later, I rang up to do just that, and to my horror, they told me he'd had to suddenly leave. I was devastated; the idea of finding a new doctor that I had to learn to trust left me full of fear.

I, of course, eventually got over it, but still, to this day, have not found someone I feel overly comfortable with. Fast forward a year, and I receive a message from him on Facebook asking how I am.

I naively saw it as just a caring old friend. He was married with children, so it never occurred to me it would be anything more. After covering the basics of where I was at, the conversation came to what I saw as a natural end. It did not end, however.

I received a message saying he was in town having a coffee if I'd like to join him. Then a message saying he'd seen me walking down the street and wanted to stop and say hi. I originally kept replying to his messages as I couldn't bring myself to accept what was happening.

My close friends made it very clear to me what he was after. One even suggested I go for it, one to tick off the bucket list and all that. But I still defended his actions.

Again, he messaged me, saying he had seen me on a night out and had wanted to come and say hi. What began to feel so weird is I never saw him. I chose to ignore this message. But a couple of days later, I decided I needed his intentions in black and white, so I could no longer pretend it was something else. The messages went as follows…

'What's with all the sudden interest?'

'Just thought it would be nice to catch up.'

'It's hardly pull-your-knickers-down kind of conversation.'

(Which he then tried to delete, but I saw this before he managed.)

'Too far?'

'Possibly.

Possibly not, you decide…'

'Well, as you're married with children, I would say yes, too far.'

'Fair enough, stay cheery.'

Now it was crystal clear, and I could no longer deny his intentions. I have a few problems with this scenario. Not only do I feel that someone I went to and who saw a great deal of my body was, in fact, looking at me in a different way, but when I first went to him, I was a pretty vulnerable person; I still can be. This position of not only power but the fact he knew so much about me has left me feeling dirty somehow. The other factor that really bothers me is that he thinks I would be the sort of person that would be OK with sleeping with a married man. I don't proclaim to be a saint, but there are definitely lines you don't cross. It may have been a completely different story if I was still drinking and using drugs, but thankfully I'm not, and I manage to keep my mistakes to a minimum.

This may have been why he left so quickly. To my knowledge, he is no longer practising medicine, and to be honest, I deleted all the messages as I didn't want a reminder of them.

But if he was doing this to me, who else was he doing it to? And who might have been too vulnerable to object?

I still get the odd message on occasion, but I now just ignore them. But I really hope that someone else hasn't had to experience this because I didn't have the strength to speak up.

The Landlord

When I first moved, it took me a little while to get settled. I started off in a hostel, then supported housing, and then to lodging a room off a professional.

Looking back, I do wonder why on earth anyone would want a 19-year-old girl lodging a room from them. My daily routine consisted of going to college and then coming back and watching reruns of Jeremy Kyle while smoking copious amounts of roll-ups and drinking coffee. Thankfully I have grown out of the Jeremy Kyle phase; I'm ashamed to say it made me feel better about this bizarre new life I had found myself in.

This man was never inappropriate and had a girlfriend who would come round, and they'd drink wine and smoke roll-ups with me while listening to music in the kitchen. I saw him as more of a father figure, and, frankly, a pretty cool one at that.

So having just been through the turmoil of the doctor situation, I receive a WhatsApp message from said landlord, asking if he could take me out for dinner or a drink. Now, this is almost 10 years after I had my last contact with him. He must have assumed I still had the same phone number and kept it in his phone, as how else would he have it? He was no longer with his girlfriend – I knew this as I was still in occasional contact with her.

Again, I'm feeling somewhat violated. So many thoughts now go through my head. Did he look at me that way when I was living with him? Was I living with someone who was secretly perving on me? Do they not get it? Or am I overreacting? How women are often made to feel ashamed when, in fact, they have done nothing wrong.

Having a bit more strength and his intentions being that bit clearer, I chose to ignore the message.

The Client

For my job, I'm pretty much paid to be nice to people for a living. Apparently, some men misread my friendliness for flirting.

By this point in the three-month period, I'm not going to lie, I was beginning to hate men in their entirety. This man would often bring me and my work colleague flowers, chocolates and similar, but some of our female clients did as well. He was pleasant enough, and I would often cut his son's hair too. He was opening up a business and needed to get a card payment terminal, so I offered to send him a link to the one I used, as if I recommended a friend, we both got a discount. This was not me giving him my number, only trying to help us both out.

However, he, of course, appeared to take it differently. He would text me for appointments, something I never did, as I liked to keep things professional and get people to call the salon directly. So, I told him this; however, this didn't stop it. When I was on holiday, he messaged me saying he wanted me to come back, as he and his son missed me. I did not reply.

Now, I don't know how many times men need to get ignored before they get the message! He then messaged me on the day I'd found out my dog I'd had with my ex had died, saying, 'You should smile more when you're walking.' He'd obviously seen me walking, and funnily enough, I can't have been looking too happy.

Never have I ever smiled more when told to smile more by a man. It's like telling someone to calm down when they're angry or telling me not to eat another biscuit. Out of stubbornness, I will never do as I'm asked.

At this point, my opinion of men has yet again crashed and burned. I'm now on the search for someone to prevent any long-lasting damage and remind me they're not all arseholes.

I am by no means what I would think a man having a midlife crisis would go for. The generic look would appear to be that of someone resembling a Barbie or similar. With pink hair and numerous tattoos, one of my closest friends' only explanation for this was that I must be like the Harley Davidson version, whereas the stereotypical women are Porsches.

Self-love

They say in order for a relationship to work, you must love yourself first. Who 'they' are, I'm not sure, but they may have a point.

Like many people today, self-love is something I've struggled with my entire life. Being the youngest of six, I constantly compared myself to my siblings, as did many other people.

I was always the quiet, shy one, too intimidated to speak up above all the other voices. This was a great disguise when it came to hiding my drug problem.

My expectations of men have always been pretty low because I believed that was all I ever deserved. When you've had this outlook on life, it can be a hard thing to change.

What's acceptable to me isn't acceptable to many others. People-pleasing definitely plays a part, always putting others' needs before my own. But is it any wonder I'm constantly failing when it comes to relationships?

When you don't believe you deserve to be happy, is it any wonder that I never am? I go from guy to guy, being completely amazed that they're slightly better than the last. Slightly better may mean simply that they don't get aggressive when they're drunk, but in fact, they do lie about almost everything.

It's something I really have to work on, but it is usually

hard to do when you're in any kind of relationship. It requires putting yourself first at all costs, my new year's resolution I made the year that I broke up with Prince Charming.

This obviously didn't last long, as I was yet again drawn into another relationship. We're told that being selfish is a bad thing; it's often used as an insult, but it shouldn't be. We need to be selfish sometimes to care for ourselves.

Putting yourself first can feel like a full-time job and takes a lot of practice to get good at. It is the epitome of self-love, though.

We live in a society that is full of comparison, and you only need to look at the latest trashy magazine to see them making money off other people's misfortune. Is it any wonder we do this to ourselves as well?

Everyone wants to be loved or even liked deep down, even if, like me, you constantly say you don't care what other people think of you. That is purely a guard you put up, scared of what people do think. So, of course, that ultimately leads to you not putting yourself first, too scared of other people's perceptions.

I walked home last night and passed the hustle and bustle of people drinking in pub gardens. Constantly aware of walking through and what others may be saying about me, not for one minute thinking that they probably hadn't even noticed me.

My mind is so hypercritical. I think I'm worthless yet have this massive ego that tells me everyone must be talking about me. When in fact, everyone is too worried about how they look or are coming across.

Knowing this has made it easier for me to dance sober; everyone is usually drunk around me and too concerned with how they look to notice whether I'm dancing like a knob. I get little glimmers of knowing this, yet other times am consumed with anxiety about how others see me.

One of my favourite films to watch to give me a bit of woman power is How to Be Single. It reminds me that you can survive this daunting world. It does not end like most films, with the leading lady finding her leading man. It finishes with the love of a great friendship.

But what if all your friends have already found their leading man? Where does that leave you?

THIS IS 30

Happily ever after

Sorry, this is not where I tell you I've met the man of my dreams and now live in the countryside with our blonde-haired, blue-eyed angels. No, I'm home alone, wishing I'd bought chocolate while I'd been out and feeling far too lazy to go out and get any.

The question is, what is happily ever after? We are mainly taught by example, so what if our example of love wasn't always that lovely?

Both my parents are happily re-married now, but growing up was not all sunshine and flowers. At times it was tough, as it is for so many families today. Not many people have parents that are still together, let alone can be in the same room as each other, so who are we meant to be emulating?

You have either the realistic albeit slightly chaotic version of family life at home or the stuff you see in the movies. Is it any wonder we're like the blind leading the blind when it comes to relationships?

Is it any wonder that we struggle to get this 'happily ever after' life when no one around us seems to have it figured out either?

We watch films, and we see people fall in love in all kinds of ways. It's like the whirlwind we all dream of, only for the film to finish when the real-life bit starts. Not even the films are helping us out here.

In today's world, everything is so confusing. We have so many choices. We could decide to identify as a tree, and well, people would have to accept it in the end. The other day I read about a woman who decided to marry herself. Nothing wrong with being a tree or marrying yourself, but all these new options can be confusing.

Others marry Paul, only years later, they are actually Pauline. People are in open relationships, swinging relationships, monogamous relationships. Am I the only one who is struggling to work out what is best for me?

When I was little, I watched Cinderella and Sleeping Beauty. I guess the idea that some gorgeous man would come and save a damsel in distress was quite appealing. Now it disgusts me. I don't want saving – I saved myself and built myself back up time and again.

I want an equal. A partner in crime. Someone I can go on adventures with, but also allows me to explore alone. Someone to grow with and fall apart with. To build a life with. Who doesn't try and tame me but embraces the madness.

I would rather be alone than settle for something that isn't right. At points of my hormone overloads and broodiness, I genuinely have started to consider getting a donor. Either that or convince my gay friend to co-parent with me.

This is the age we live in; nothing is off limits anymore, so who's to say I can't be with a man called Brendan, who was Bree, who's just given birth to a child fathered by Matt, who's in an open relationship with Mark, who's married to Sue.

And amongst all these examples of love, I'm somehow meant to work out how to make a relationship work while causing as little damage to my future offspring as possible.

Maybe I should get another dog and more Ben and Jerry's.

Thirty

That number we seem to dread. Through my teens and twenties, I never thought ageing would happen to me – do any of us? Part of that was due to being intoxicated and romanticising the fact I'd be dead at twenty-seven like so many famous souls. But it wasn't to be. I was supposed to reach this number, sober and single(ish) and with no real plan of what the fuck I'm meant to be doing.

My walk to work takes me a matter of minutes. I walk through the same underpass every day and look over the array of new belongings and graffiti that it has been decorated with from the previous night. A new bit of graffiti had been sprayed on the brick wall saying, 'Where are my people?' and I really felt that. A week or so later, it seemed the council had decided to do a tidy-up, that same bit of graffiti washed away from the wall. It looked cleaner than I'd ever seen it. By the afternoon, someone had decided to drop a dozen eggs on the floor... that is what being thirty feels like.

Before, when I would stay the night somewhere, I'd take makeup wipes, maybe some moisturiser and a few bits of makeup. Now when I go away, I feel like I need a whole bag for the lotions and potions that claim to rejuvenate my skin. Face wash, toner, facial oil, moisturiser, eye cream, plus makeup. Then it's a whole different routine for the evening, face wash, toner, night balm, eye cream, eyelash serum, and some crystal roller that does lymphatic drainage, although I'm still not quite sure what that means. I had never stepped foot in a beautician's before my mid-twenties. I was always pretty low maintenance, but it seems the older you get, the more high maintenance you become. There's eyebrow tinting and shaping, eyelash lifting and tinting, lasering to stop those dreaded ingrown hairs, manicures, and not to mention facials. I've tried almost everything on my skin over the years to combat breakouts, and facials seem to be the one thing that works, but then there's the expensive lotions and potions that all come at a price and seem to be the only products that don't aggravate it, leaving you looking like a pubescent teenager.

Every day I seem to notice a new line or wrinkle or that dreaded chin hair. I mean, seriously, what is that about? I'm naturally fair, yet I get a jet-black chin hair sprouting its ugly head to add to what is already a difficult day. Then there's the pigmentation that comes out like a dark moustache every time I go in the sun, caused by being on a contraceptive pill without being warned I should stay out of the sun. Someone even commented on my 'tache' once, leaving me to go and spend over a hundred pounds on a makeup counter to try and hide all my god-awful marks on my face. I have to say there's nothing like an insecure woman to make a shitload of commission when you're working on a beauty counter. The number of times I've been on the edge of tears asking to be made 'beautiful' and, in turn, spending more than my monthly mortgage payment is an actual joke.

It seems endless; this morning, I noticed a new line on my forehead and instantly took a picture with arrows pointing to it to my friend, the caption reading, 'What the actual fuck'. I've seen these silicone patches you can get online to wear when you sleep that are meant to rejuvenate your skin and remove fine lines and wrinkles, as well as prevent them. Do I buy into more of this marketing? But then, if I was to buy these, not only would I be wearing a silk hat (don't knock it – it's great for your hair, but not exactly attractive), a mouth guard to stop me grinding and ultimately chipping my teeth, and now patches of silicone? Am I just never going to share a bed with anyone again? Can you imagine the look on their faces when you get into bed? It will be like something out of a horror movie!

My social media reels are now full of people with children, getting married, or their growing baby bump, as opposed to people on nights out and at festivals. Both give you that dreaded FOMO but in different ways. Thankfully no one is travelling at the moment, so at least we're all in the same boat in that sense. I never thought in a million years my thirtieth year would be spent not only sober and single but social distancing as well. With no appetite for dating and finally at a point where my own company is precious, it all seems a bit surreal. The time when you're single is meant to be that of dancing and spending time with your girlfriends. This year seems to be a slightly wasted one, but one that I am still ageing!

When I was in Pamplona alone and feeling lost on the last day of my Camino, I saw a print in a shop window that said, 'You own your life'. It's so easy to forget this and get caught up in the madness. It's true, though – we do. No one is coming to save us. How we live our life is one hundred per cent our responsibility. I'm not about to let all the bullshit drag me down.

As David Bowie said...

'I don't know where I'm going from here, but I promise it won't be boring.'

Phone call to my friend

Hysterically crying

'What've you done?'

'Getting older is a trap, I hate men, why do I always pick the wrong people? I'm getting wrinkly, my boobs are sagging, my vagina will sag! It's a trap, getting older is a trap, I don't want to get any fucking older! If I see one more post about someone being pregnant or getting married or about their fucking kids, I'm gonna break my phone! I've got a top with drawings of tits on, and my boobs are lower than the ones on the T-shirt! Why do I always fall in love with people that can't offer me what I want!!?? Why does everyone else find it easier than meee!'

(All whilst sobbing and wiping snot on my clothes)

'Who finds it easier?'

'Everyone, everyone has their life together and I'm falling apart, I'm gonna have to buy these fucking silicone patches cos I'm getting old. I'm more likely to marry my friend than find a man I want to spend the rest of my life with. I hate them all! I hate them, I hate them, I hate them! I'm going to die alone, surrounded by dogs! I'm gonna get fat and saggy and ugly!'

'You know your body will change if you have kids?'

'Yes, but at least I'll have something to show for it! The reason my body looks a mess! I'm just gonna have a saggy vagina for no reason!'

'Maybe you should be kinder to yourself, treat yourself how you would treat me.'

'Aaarrrgggghhhh'

(More uncontrollable sobbing)

My friends deserve awards!

Lockdown

No one in their right mind ever thinks they will live through a global pandemic. There are films that involve zombie apocalypses and everyone's fantasy worst-case scenario, but not many of us actually believe we will live through one.

2020 was meant to be my year. Having up to this point had slightly disastrous years, I was convinced this new decade was going to be different, the time everything was finally going to fall into place.

I was turning thirty, no longer able to convince myself I was still a teenager, like, for some reason, I had for the last ten years. No, I was a proper adult. I had a year planned of exciting holidays, evenings out and festivals, and then Covid came into the world and messed it all up.

I count myself as one of the lucky ones, I really do. I personally have not had to experience anyone dying as a result of Covid. However, my life did somewhat turn on its head, and the year that was meant to be the start of the rest of my life has been one of the most trying to date.

I was lucky enough to go on holiday just before lockdown came into place. There were whispers of it before I went, but ever convinced this year was going to be great, I did not for one minute think it was going to become my reality. Whereas most people had a warming-up period to lockdown, my sister and I flew back to England only days before the whole country was shut down. While we were away, our close friends and family advised us to self-isolate on our return, so we went into our own lockdown almost instantly.

Now, I am the first person who will moan about working, I do love my job, but at times, it can be challenging. Working with the general public is not always easy, although sometimes it does have its benefits. I had gone on holiday and acted as if I had just won the lottery, as I often do because I'm not one to penny pinch when I'm abroad. As far as I'm concerned, I work hard and I deserve to enjoy myself, but coming back from this to the prospect of not working for I don't know how long was not ideal.

On the Monday night, the whole of the country was told they mustn't go out unless completely necessary. You were not allowed to see other households and were only to go out for one hour of exercise a day. I felt like I'd gone back in time to where my anxiety had been so bad after splitting with an ex that I had barely left the confines of my flat.

I often say I'd love to be a kept woman, but would I? With a total of four months off work, I've come to realise I don't do well without a routine. Without any children to occupy my time, I would wake up every morning wondering what on earth to do. I had, of course, decided to lock down with somebody, and thank God I did because, frankly, without them there, I'm sure I would have had a mental breakdown. What was meant to be a casual one night of passion, from me sliding into his DMs, led to a relationship that neither of us was happy to call 'a relationship'. Thinking that 'lockdown' would last a couple of weeks, we both decided to live in my flat together.

Throughout my life, like so many, I have suffered from

mental health problems. I do my best not to let them take over my life but have realised now more than ever that working is a great medicine for me. Waking up every morning with a purpose and having to put a smile on my face, even if it's fake, has its advantages. It takes you out of your head and you almost go into a different role. When you're at home, however, there is no need to put on this fake smile and play this role. I found my bad days often turned into bad weeks, as I never had any reason to get out of them.

I, like many, painted everything in sight, had bouts of doing exercise daily and cooking elaborate meals I would never usually have bothered to do. But I also had many days where I would stare into space, not talk, or only talk to request some more chocolate from the shop.

Not being able to see family was another struggle for me. On my thirtieth birthday, I woke up to find my living room decorated with balloons and confetti; he really had done his best to make it somewhat special, but not being able to see my family and friends, I found it extremely hard. Frankly, I have to say, even given the circumstances, this was one of the better birthdays I'd had in years. I guess I can thank my exes for this – they had been able to ruin quite a number of them.

I was desperate for things to go back to normal, but even six months on, there isn't much hope of this happening. It's like we're living in a movie, everyone in shops wearing masks and still no prospect of hugging our loved ones anytime soon.

It has been a testing time for so many of us, and I have to be grateful for the fact I don't live in a high-rise building with no outside space. People have not only died from

Covid; I know of at least three people that have committed suicide during this time, and it seems to be something that is being brushed under the carpet.

I have learnt to appreciate my family and friends a lot more. Over the past few years, I have found every excuse under the sun to avoid seeing my family at Christmas. I struggle with so many strong personalities in one place. This year I'm going to find some strength from deep down inside of me and try not to embrace my usual Scrooge persona. I'm extremely lucky to have the family I do, even if they, at times, drive me to the brink of insanity. Who knows how many Christmases I will have left with them? No one ever thought something like this would happen, and I need to remember to appreciate the people I have in my life.

When I had well and truly run out of things to occupy myself with, I had my friend in my ear telling me to write. She had for so long been trying to persuade me to write a book. I have never thought of myself as particularly bright or academic, constantly comparing myself to my older siblings who'd managed to make it to university. If anything, I thought, maybe one day I could let my grandchildren read it so they could realise I haven't always been an old woman.

With every chapter I've written, I've felt some sort of pride in myself. Originally, I was too embarrassed to let anyone read it, but have pushed myself to let people see my true self.

I've learnt you have to push yourself in this life and do things out of your comfort zone that you may never have even dreamt of.

My mum always tried to teach us the best things in life are

free; she always encouraged us to look at nature, listen to birdsong. Growing up, I generally found this embarrassing, but she's got a point. When life is nothing like you've ever known it to be, you have to slow down and appreciate the little things in life that we so often take for granted: the sun shining, the laughter of a friend, the touch of a loved one.

Maybe my life was meant to take this turn – without lockdown, would I have ever tried to write, something I now find so cathartic? I've had to find something that costs nothing to get me through this time. Maybe it will never be read by anyone else, and that's OK.

With the world consumed by things that cost money to gratify us all, I feel happy that I've finally found joy in something that costs nothing.

Maybe the best things in life are, in fact, free.

Adulting

How have I managed to get to adulthood? It seems only days ago I was in the school playground talking about boys with my friends and trying to learn what wanking meant.

I was definitely a slow developer, in every way. I was the last of my friends to grow any boobs, and frankly, I'm still waiting for them. Although I was the youngest of six, I was extremely naive when it came to anything to do with boys or sex.

My sex talk with my mum was less of a talk and more of a passing comment, telling me not to make mistakes like she had. And there I was, thrown into the adult world, still not having a clue what she meant.

I remember vividly going out with a boy in school – I'm not sure if we ever even kissed – and deciding I didn't like him anymore. I asked one of my friends to go and break up with him for me, a situation I now wish in adulthood was socially acceptable.

How do you know if you're making the right decision? A decision that seemed to come to me so easily is now a constant bout of anxiety and overthinking. The thing is, it's no longer a case of whether you like someone – there are a million other questions that now cross my mind that never did in my younger years.

Now knowing I would like to have that family, something I never thought I did, is both a blessing and a curse. I can no longer rely on my feelings for someone or my attraction to them. No, now I have to ask myself, 'Do I see a future with them?'

Reaching thirty has seemed like a pinnacle event. No longer can I hide behind being twenty-something, foot-loose and fancy-free. Although many people start their families in their late thirties or early forties these days, it's not a sure thing.

At the age of 25, your odds of conceiving after three months of trying are just under 20%. By age 35, your odds of conceiving after three months of trying are about 12%. Ok, I'm as shocked as you are by this, as I just googled it. What the fuck! Thanks, healthline.com...

I mean, is that not terrifying? Yes, of course, it can happen, but it's not only society telling us we must meet the one and have a family – it's science.

So now, when I'm dating someone, I dissect their whole being. Do we have the same outlook on life, the same morals, the same idea of how we'd bring up a family? It's no longer enough to just really like them.

And then comes the part I find the hardest, ending it with them because of this. I'm an empath through and through and often put other people's feelings before my own. I'm used to being unhappy, so I would rather be unhappy and make someone else happy. But am I?

Am I actually making this other person happy, or am I wasting their time? I think I'm doing it to please them, but actually, am I just being a coward?

I look around me, and my friends seem to have it sorted; their decisions seem to be more, 'What shall I make my child for breakfast?' rather than, 'Who should I spend my life with?'

They seem to do it all so organically, and maybe that's the thing – if it's not organic, it's not right. But you grow attached to these relationships, you get comfortable in them, and saying your truth seems so hard.

If I was younger, I know I wouldn't feel so much pressure to end relationships that weren't right; maybe that's how I've not spent a Christmas single in about 15 years. Now seems like the time I've got to really knuckle down and find out what I want and don't want.

I'm fortunate that most other areas in my life are pretty good. I have a job I love, in a place I love. I'm on the property ladder, albeit with a lot of help from my parents. I finally can say I have a good group of friends who I love and trust. But in every other way possible, I feel a complete wreck.

More often than not, I eat chocolate for my dinner or have a ready meal that I eat directly out of the tub to avoid more washing up. And the world is telling me this person has the responsibility to make choices for herself and how her life should go?

It is my responsibility, though, and however hard it is, I must now make these decisions that I try so hard to avoid. I can no longer ask my friend to break up with a boy for me and must find some inner strength to do it myself.

Not seeing a future with someone has now become a good enough reason to end it.

Adulting for me is like wanting to cry for four days but not having the time.

Break-ups, make-ups & fuck-ups

It's been a month since I ended my latest 'relationship' – if I can, in fact, call it that – although there have been a few slip-ups. I am human, after all! I tend to go into complete meltdown, rebelling in any way I can – although these days, my idea of rebellion is quite pathetic. Where I was expected to eat a proper dinner, my rebellion is eating ice cream instead. The first few weeks, I was eating as little as possible; this past month, I've basically practised absolutely no self-care. Self-care starts from the inside out, and I've now reached a point where I'm bored of my own whining. I am in charge of my life, and filling my body with shit is not going to make me feel good. I tend to sleep at every given opportunity to avoid my feelings, as changing them with substances is no longer an option and would be catastrophic. But there is only so much feeling sorry for yourself you can do. The world is shit enough at the minute without adding to it with the dramas of my romantic life. It's time to take action. If I want to buy the fucking silicone pads, I will. If small stupid things like that and eating vegetables as opposed to copious amounts of chocolate will make me feel better, I'm all for it.

How do we get here? Why does it seem with every break-up, you feel even more hurt and guarded? I managed to get out of work early, worried I may cry on my unsuspecting clients. We're currently experiencing a heat wave, added to which we're going through a global pandemic which is forcing us all to wear PPE.

Crying and sweating whilst trying to stay upbeat and

cheery is too much for me today. Feeling like I want to get home asap without seeing anyone or them seeing my swollen and bloodshot eyes, I run to the newsagents across the road to grab some dinner. Dinner is, of course, three Magnums, with no sign of anything that remotely resembles any kind of vegetable.

But apparently, I'm not suffering enough, no. Before being able to hide my dinner, I bump straight into 'The Young One'. He, of course, knows I do not have kids or anyone else at home that could be somehow helping me eat all this ice cream. I guess it could have been worse, I could have been coming out of the sex shop next door with three new vibrators.

So here I am at home with the fan on full, in my pants and bra, crying, eating one Magnum after another and writing about how I've managed to get myself in this god-awful situation again. I genuinely do not want any straight cock near me right now. How many tears do I have to cry, how many break-ups do I have to go through before I find the 'one', believing, of course, that they exist?

My meals from now on will no doubt be brown in colour and full of sugar. My roll-up consumption has increased as if I'm trying to mimic Madge off *Benidorm*. No doubt, if I continue on this diet, I may need an electric scooter too!

With every heartbreak, I feel an extra wall is put up in what feels to me is now a fortress. Will anyone be able to get through it? I have a hard enough time understanding myself, so how is anyone else meant to?

So, I call in my friends, the ones that have made it or have at least conquered some of my life goals. First in line is one part of my throuple. Now I know it's a shameful thing to admit, but sometimes it is hard to be around my friends like this. When they have everything you want and are trying so hard to find, is it any wonder the green-eyed monster comes into play?

She's only months away from completing her family, and although this comes with challenges of its own, I can't help but be jealous. My problems sometimes seem so insignificant, not that I'm ever made to feel this way, but how does another heartbreak really compare to bringing a new life into the world? To being told that you may not have the birth you planned? Because of something to do with the placenta being in the wrong place, she may actually have to have a caesarean. Now she's looking at the possibility of having her stomach cut open, and here I am crying over yet another man.

Now with most fights, you make up – not technically true in my case, but it's what I'm told. Then comes the all-important make-up sex, usually full of passion – you're more often than not just getting your anger out towards this person in a pleasurable way.

Some people I've known have initiated arguments just to get these passionate few minutes. But what if there is no argument and you actually decide to break up on civil ground? Can you still have the passion, or does it just go to platonic?

Do we ever know if we haven't, in fact, fucked up? I feel like I've often got so many voices in my head telling me different things that it's hard to work out what's actually good for me. Can you come back from a fuck-up? Can relationships actually be better after you've broken up or someone's had an affair?

Maybe I've got some more research to do to find out the answers to all these questions, or maybe I could just ask other people. I'm not sure how much my heart can take.

Everyone in their own right has their struggles, whether it's to do with their families or the fact they don't have one. If I've learnt one thing, it is that break-ups don't, in fact, need to have people screaming and shouting. Yes, it's not as easy as getting your friend to do it when you're fourteen, but if you love and respect someone, you can at least be kind.

That does, however, bring a whole other issue. If there is no screaming and shouting, no smashing of mirrors, no stealing of cars, nothing explosive to make yourself feel confident that this is exactly the right thing to do, how do you know it is?

Is it just another fuck-up?

No doubt this will not be my last break-up, make-up or fuck-up. With each time, another wall may go up, but I will also learn from it. I will learn what I want and don't want and hopefully be more content being on my own.

Usually, I'm ready to do my usual and get under someone sharpish. This time feels different, maybe it's time I went without, and maybe I won't keep making the same mistakes if I had more time to reflect. Less time hunting down my next prey, who, in all honesty, is just distracting me from the emptiness I feel.

Fuck... am I actually becoming an adult!?

I am not a nun

This, I'm sure, comes as no surprise to you – you've read the previous chapters – but the men in my life seem to treat me as such. It would appear that because I don't do drugs, I am unable to see the signs, that because I don't cheat, I never have cheated. I am, in fact, a naive child that has not lived at all.

I've often used the phrase, 'Don't bullshit a bullshitter', once to a girl who was clearly trying it on with my boyfriend at the time – who I had started seeing behind someone else's back. I'm not proud of my younger years, but it has prepared me for the harsh reality that is life. I've lied, I've cheated, I've taken drugs, and lied some more to cover up most of my actual existence. Since stopping all of this soul-destroying behaviour, it seems the universe has gifted me with the inability to lie anymore or lie well, at least. When attempting to lie, I generally turn the colour of a beetroot, smile, look down, all the obvious signs that any person could pick up on. This is a blessing and a curse; it enables me to live a pretty honest existence, but don't ask me if your bum looks big in those jeans if you don't want the honest answer.

You are told to trust your gut; everyone has had that gnawing feeling that something is amiss. There's the time your boyfriend stays out all night, says he stayed at his friend's and that he just dropped him off. When his phone goes off a couple of minutes later and you ask who it is, he claims it's the same friend asking if he got home OK. Maybe that wasn't a gut situation, maybe that was being caught out, but he fed me a web of lies and made me feel like I was insane. Nearly a year later, I found out he'd cheated on me that night and had stayed at a girl's house only months after we'd bought a flat together.

Then there are the times when your 'friends' try to hide the fact they're taking drugs from you. People seem to think I'm anti-drugs – I'm not. If anything, I'm pro-drugs – drugs are just not pro-me. They sneak off to the toilet together, do dodgy handshakes, come out sniffing and wiping their noses. I don't have anything against people taking drugs; I mean, my exes seemed to love them, just have the respect to not do it around me. I've always been upfront and honest with people, do what you like, but if you're going on a mad one, do it when I'm not around. I would love nothing more than to jump on that bus with you, but where it takes me is a very sad, lonely place, and I don't need the temptation around me when I would do anything to escape my feelings.

It still astounds me how they just don't seem to get it, and what's worse, they can lie so convincingly to your face. You can see all the signs – the massive pupils, the sneaking around, them not getting out of bed until the afternoon because they're exhausted from work. And I buy it, time and time again. This is what love can do to you; it makes you stupid, wanting to believe the bullshit and losing yourself in the process.

When I start to date someone, I lay my cards on the table. If you do drugs, that's fine, but I don't want to date you. Pretty straightforward, you'd think. Apparently not. It's not like I let them get invested in me first, it's just something I don't want in a relationship. And they all say the same thing, 'I used to dabble, but never anything heavy, I've grown up since then.' But they haven't, and it's like they're laying the foundations for their future lies.

So, I find myself in the same situation for what seems like the hundredth time. I've already caught this particular person out months earlier. When you're sober and someone is coked up when you're having sex, it's pretty obvious. When you're sober, most things are pretty obvious. I'm one of the most understanding people I know; this isn't me being arrogant, but it's a great bugbear for many of my friends. If people are honest with me, I can deal with it. I might not be happy, but I'll get over it. So, I was throwing shapes in the bedroom with this particular individual when I noticed he was obviously on something. All of a sudden, they get experimental, start asking you things they would never dare if they weren't high. And so, I ask them straight out, not angry, not annoyed, and they always say no. Then they go to the bathroom for the fifth time in ten minutes, so I open the door, praying that they don't have the shits but knowing that my gut is always right. There they are, huddled over the toilet with a banknote and credit card, almost annoyed that you've dared walk into your own bathroom. Then the row starts, and the sex stops.

I feel I have a right to be slightly dubious. I've spent months on end with this person and know their every quirk. We've heard each other shit, fart, and seen every part of each other's bodies. So, it's safe to say I know him pretty well. At this point, we've technically broken up, but as in many relationships, he's been coming round for a booty call, no doubt delaying the inevitable, another break-up within the break-up. He's three hours late, and by this time, I'm starting to wonder if I've made a mistake, and maybe we could see how things go with us. When he finally arrives, he's straight down to business. No kissing, barely a word shared between us, but it's different this time. I see his face in the mirror and he's gurning; my heart sinks, and I try to fight back the tears. He runs out to get his smokes, and I know it's only a matter of time before I can no longer hide the tears dripping down my face. There's nothing quite like sex to help stop you from crying, or so I thought. He puts his fingers in my mouth and I taste coke, my mouth feels numb. Is this really happening to me again? So, I ask him, but he denies it and tries to carry on. I plead with him not to treat me like an idiot, and eventually, he leaves, telling me he hadn't come over for this bullshit.

Case closed? If only. I ring my sister, crying, 'Why does this always happen to me!?' Hysterically, I tell her the undiluted version. The next day I'm heartbroken – it's like they're chasing the dragon, and I'm the dragon. He calls round later, smiling ear to ear, telling me I made a mistake. That it's no big deal. I believe him, even sending him a message later apologising for accusing him. That night I lay in my bed, going over it again and again. I've never been wrong; every time my gut has told me something's up, it has been. I have just usually chosen to ignore it and believe them. He asks to come round later that night, and I explain I'm having trouble making sense of what happened. He's blasé, he reiterates that I just got it wrong. When I ask him to explain his behaviour, he deflects and eventually tells me he doesn't have time for this drama. I don't reply.

The end? No, because I'm a slave to any man that shows me any kind of love. He messages me later, saying he doesn't want to leave it like this, can he come round. I'm thinking that it's better we part on good terms, so I agree. Again, he turns up bold as brass. He tells me again I've got it wrong. This time he is the person I remember, he's got that aftershave on he knows I like, his smile melts me.

Before long, we're back in my bedroom, getting the tension out on each other. But nothing's changed – I'm just even more confused than I was before. I tell him this and he leaves.

Could I be wrong? Does your gut lie to you? Had I imagined the whole thing?

So many times, I have ignored my better judgement. I've let my heart lead and not my head. The horrible thing is I'll never know for sure; it's his word against mine. But I'm more important. Regardless of whether I'm bat-shit crazy, I can't unfeel how I felt. It's just one time too many for me. Please go and do a mountain of drugs, sleep with whoever you want, tell all the lies you want. Just leave me at the bus stop; don't take me on the bus.

I've been made to feel like I'm going mad so many times that I can no longer tell the difference. In life, you have one person you need to look after more than anyone, and it's yourself. So, whether I'm right or I'm wrong, it seems clear to me I'm not ready to trust someone like I should.

A relationship without trust is like a car without petrol: you can stay in it, but it won't go anywhere.

Timing

Everything is about timing. For as long as I can remember, I've found myself in a relationship. This has never been an intentional thing, more something I've just become used to. I genuinely don't have a problem being on my own; actually, I quite like having my own space. I used to think a man completed me when in fact, I had to complete myself.

Can it be the right person at the wrong time? This is something I'm never quite sure of. If it was the right person, surely it would always be the right time. Or is that just how these things are portrayed in films? I've found many times feelings for others have intruded on relationships I'm in. They say the grass is always greener, but that depends on which side you're watering it.

When you're going through a shit time in a relationship, it's often easy to romanticise someone else. Let's face it – the beginnings of all relationships are fun, although often stress-inducing in my case. You laugh and joke getting to know one another and generally don't have anything to argue about. So, of course, it always seems like the better option, but we can't just constantly date people for a couple of months only to give up when it all gets serious.

I know at this point in my life, I really should be alone. I know I need to work on myself and make sure I'm doing things for the right reason rather than to fill the void I feel with sex. I need to spend a Christmas alone. I need to remind myself of what I like doing and the things that bring me joy.

Depending on where you live, this can be a struggle. One of my older sisters lives in London, where the majority of her friends are single. At this moment in time, I don't have one friend that doesn't have either a boyfriend/husband or kids, with some having both.

You end up comparing yourself; how can I be so far re-moved from where my friends are? Part of me wants all that, but I know deep down I'm not ready.

Added to this, you have people constantly asking you about your relationship status. Then reassuring you not to worry, you will find that man of your dreams. Whatever happened to people just asking if you were happy, rather than basing your happiness on whether you have a part-ner or a good job? Some of us are happiest when we are single but get made to feel like we shouldn't be.

I remember one of my friends who was single at the time saying that when he looked at couples, instead of feeling envious, he'd be pleased he wouldn't have to watch some boring chick flick that evening and was able to watch and do whatever he pleased without having to compromise.

Your social life is then dictated by whether your friends can get childcare or, God forbid, have other friends that they want to hang out with. You end up feeling very iso-lated and alone, realising the only single people you can meet are on Tinder but are often there to find some sort of relationship rather than a new friend to hang out with.

Maybe if I'm alone too long, I will become very selfish and struggle to let someone in on my routine, and ultimately end up that spinster that my father fears so much.

I know I've had my heart broken more times than I care to count, and I have ultimately resorted to being an ice queen. I can date until I'm blue in the face, but if I'm unable to get vulnerable and let someone really see me, the timing just isn't right.

How to stay single

This is not a chapter where I tell you how to stay single, but more a baffling question I seem to be asking myself. People often look at others who have been in constant relationships as if they've got a secret to managing this. I, however, feel the secret seems to lie in being a pushover and expecting very little.

This is something I've constantly battled with. I have on numerous occasions stated to my friends that this is genuinely what I want, only ever managing it for a couple of weeks. Last night I met two of my friends to yet again proclaim I wanted to be single until at least New Year's Day.

They, of course, met my statement with a bit of a cynical look. They know me better than most, having worked with me for many years and knowing I all too often fall into dicksand. I've finally realised that I cannot date successfully and stay single. If I want to stay single, I need to practise abstinence from men. No texting, no flirting, no dating, and no meeting up.

I'm sure they both want to hit my head against a brick wall, as they seem to see me so differently from how I see myself. Having experienced every high and low with me in the last decade, they've become fiercely protective of me and, at points, extremely frustrated.

A lot of people hate going out with someone that's sober, but these two relish it. I'm able to be a taxi, and for one, help pull her pants up on a night out when she's had far too much Prosecco and can't quite work out how to manage that without toppling over onto the piss-stained floor of the club toilets.

We're currently living in a world that feels like zombies could come out at any time. It's 2020, the year that so many of us were sure would be the best year ever. In reality, it's been a bit of a shitter. Covid 19 has a lot to answer for; weddings, birthdays and all celebrations have been cancelled. People have died without their loved ones by their side, and we've had to practise social distancing instead of dancing.

I feel to achieve my new single status, I need to enlist the help of my friends. I've already told many of them that if I even mention dating, they all have permission to tit-punch me. It's like I need constant bouncers around me to stop myself. On those dark lonely nights when my friends are cooking dinners for their families or spending time with their partners, I need to learn to not feel lonely.

I've already started my plans by watching *How to Be Single* as well as singing loudly to 'Survivor' by Destiny's Child. How hard can it be? My first weekend in my now single status, I've decided to escape to my mum's, with no temptation in sight. I can spend my time going to the gym, seeing my loved ones as well as trying to become a best-selling author. I guess it's always good to dream.

My mother's already suggested I join a rambling club. For those that don't know this, it's a walking club that is no doubt filled with retired folk. Is there perhaps a chastity belt I can purchase? Maybe my dad actually has one somewhere. Or maybe the trick is to stop maintaining areas that would be seen in these circumstances. Maybe I should go back to my homeless look and bring back the resting bitch face.

I remember watching *40 Days and 40 Nights*, where Josh Hartnett plays a character practising abstinence from women. He struggled all the way through, but in the end, he met a girl and they lived happily ever after, at least the bits we saw. I'm planning on doing this for 142 days with very little experience.

There doesn't appear to be a handy app for giving up relationships like there is for giving up smoking. Is this a market they're missing out on in the app department? After googling 'giving up relationship app' all I'm greeted with are links to dating apps or articles written by people that have deleted dating apps. Why is there no help for people wanting to stay single?

I've now not taken drugs for nearly 12 years; surely I can give up men. Maybe this pandemic is actually a blessing in disguise. I'm really trying to find the positives in all this. It is almost impossible to date people at the moment if you abide by the strict rules that are in place. Obviously, many people aren't following the rules, but maybe if I did, then I could actually feel some gratitude towards the government for helping me on my path to enlightenment.

And so, my rehabilitation has begun, and this time I really hope I don't fall off the waggon.

Dicksand

Unfortunately, this is not a phrase I can take credit for. It was taken from my go-to film, *How to Be Single*. It is meant to be like quicksand – once you're in, it's hard to get out, but in the form of men. This is very much a reality for me.

I'm less than a week into my supposed abstinence, and it seems I've already fallen off the waggon. My most recent ex came to 'collect some of his things' when it seems it was an excuse to see me. Of course, I was a sucker for him. I had not ended this relationship because anything bad had happened or that I no longer liked him, but we seem to be on very different paths.

So there I went and fell into his dicksand. I'd missed his smell, his touch, his everything, and frankly didn't take much persuading. But then reality hit us both the following day. I think he had expected to stay again, whilst I had to explain nothing had changed.

This seems to be men's kryptonite. Be unavailable, be hard to get, and they will want you more. That phrase I hate, 'Treat them mean to keep them keen' seems to be true. I never intentionally do this; however, I wear my heart on my sleeve, often to my detriment. But the more I keep pushing people away, the more they want me. If only I'd been able to act like this on every occasion I was being dumped by the most recent love of my life.

I rang a friend to explain my most recent predicament,

saying how I was also trying to stop myself from contacting some different dicksand to move me on. Listening to myself, I cringed, I sounded like a spoilt princess of cock. Even the other day, a friend had sarcastically said how awful it must be knowing there are numerous men out there wanting to sleep with you.

I get that we're in the middle of a global pandemic, and I should be grateful. When I was in India, a woman tried to convince me that men's penises were 'the light' and we should be grateful for receiving them – I'm not so sure about this. Yes, they can be great, but they also come with a lot of complications that I'm currently trying to stay clear of.

I even contemplated that maybe I should revisit my experimental youth and date women for a few months. My friend reminded me that was still sex and maybe I should try a couple of weeks without it, and if I reach that milestone, try another couple. It appears, given my history, not everyone is convinced I'm going to make it to New Year's Day.

I guess I just love to love, in all shapes and forms. 'What is life without love' (more *Friends* quotes, I'm sorry!), but seriously – what is life without love?

So, I didn't make it to a full week, but I'm going to dust myself off and start again. I need to do this for me, I need to stop trying to fill this hole, pun intended, with dicksand. If at first, you don't succeed, try try, try again!

When something isn't enriching your life and only blurring your path, there is only so long people will listen to you moan about it. I need to learn how to fill the void without the help of anyone else and work out who I really am and what I really want.

So, I will jump over the dicksand, wear blinkers when I go out and avoid contacting anyone of the opposite sex unless it's a family member or they're gay.

Fuck you, dicksand, I'm not falling into that again.

Under pressure

'Everyone you meet asks if you've got a career, are married, or own a house as if life were some kind of grocery list. But no one ever asks if you are happy.'

Wise words from the legend Heath Ledger

It's time I caught up with one part of my throuple. While in the middle of a global pandemic, socialising has been somewhat problematic. As she's pregnant and I'm now back working, social distancing has become ever more important.

We decide to meet at her local park. My only memory of parks is going as a teenager to drink whatever alcohol we could get hold of, smoke weed and kiss boys. My experience is slightly different these days.

A local woman that is on the park committee – yes, apparently that is a thing – approaches us to talk about a fundraiser to help get new equipment for the park. My beautiful friend is glowing and about six months pregnant, with her angelic boy in tow. I, of course, am alone. The lady asks if I have children. At this point, I think referring to my dog child wouldn't be an appropriate response, so I reply, 'No.' She then says, 'Never mind' in a tone that I can only describe as pity.

Now, this really is a pet hate of mine. Why do you pity me or feel sorry for me because I don't have children? Like I've passed my sell-by date, I am fucked, and no one could possibly impregnate me now.

Too often, I have people judge me for not having two point four children and a husband, for not having reached a point in my life that society tells me is appropriate for my age.

When talking to clients, they're often keen to hear about my personal life. Comments like, 'Don't worry, you'll meet your Prince Charming' or, 'There's someone out there for everyone' just confirms that more and more people do not think your life is complete unless it is conventional.

Of course, I would like to meet this mysterious man who could apparently complete my life, but I actually quite like my life. I like not having to compromise my wants and needs for someone else's. I like watching whatever I like on the tv, I like wearing big granny pants and not shaving my legs.

Why is this seen as such a bad thing!?

The only thing that this does is make you question your life and feel like you're missing out. This only leads to you missing out on the present and the fun you're having in that moment.

Who is anyone to judge how you live your life? I try my best to have an open mind to however people decide to live or who they decide to be. I wish that people would treat me with the same kindness.

Social media - a blessing or a curse?

Apparently, this is the world we now live in, where a memory isn't a memory unless it's posted on social media. Where we rely on how many likes we get or how many have tuned in to look at our stories.

I'm grateful that during my younger years, it wasn't quite so popular. This being said, there is still an active Myspace page with some photos I'm no longer proud to represent who I am, but no way of removing it as I no longer remember the password for 'prinzezlollipop'. I guess it could be worse.

Is a photo really a photo without being edited or having filters on it? I studied photography for two years, although most of that time I was wasted, but that's where the real art comes out, is it not? I always preferred film photography to digital, which was still a relatively new gadget. I like the candid photos, the ones in those throw-away cameras that you got the joy of seeing for the first time when your film was developed.

Nothing seems to be candid anymore, though. I hold my hands up to being part of this ever-growing fake world. For every photo I decide to upload, there are at least twenty that didn't make the cut. The wrong lighting, I look fat in that, you can see my spots, I look tired, I look ugly, the list is endless. I seem to forget that all those photos are, in fact, me.

I'm not sure if it's because the photo quality is so much

clearer these days compared to the days of film or the fact we now have every editing app at our fingertips. I had to delete one of my social media apps as there was a beautifying filter, and I realised I was comparing my normal face to how it looked in these photos without ever being able to reach this level of what I deemed 'beautiful' or at least my level of it.

Thankfully I have not gone as far as to completely change my appearance beyond recognition. Some people do. I saw a news article about a couple of influencers and the comparison to their real selves and their social media selves. They were beyond recognition. They had changed every part of their bodies and faces to create what they saw as perfect. Is this who we want to be influencing us?

I took a much-needed social media hiatus when I found out my beloved dog I had with my ex had died. Apparently, this is how we find out these days as opposed to being told directly. This completely broke me, and I decided I didn't want to be part of this world.

Unfortunately, in my line of work, you need a presence. You can showcase your work and gain new clients – it's free advertising. So, after a little while, I decided to go back to this world, trying my best to eliminate people who no longer added to my well-being.

Thankfully there are now ways to mute people without having to, God forbid, unfriend them. There are so many politics attached to all this that you try to not look petty or hurt people's feelings for the fear of being judged or disliked.

Being single and being on social media obviously has its perks, especially if you've given up on the dating apps. Slipping into people's DMs or showing interest by following a complete stranger has now become the new normal. You can hide behind your respective screen without having to put yourself out there in public. Being turned down in private seems to be more manageable. You are also able to stay in contact or get back in contact with all those people you hadn't bothered to keep in touch with, but now it seems weird if you're not friends on Facebook with Becky that you played with when you were four.

A lot of the time, it is used for being nosy. You can look up your ex and see what they're up to, how much happier they are without you, or, better still, how fucked up they look now you're no longer in their lives.

To me, it's like self-harm. What am I really doing when I'm scrolling through? I'm comparing myself to what I know deep down isn't someone's reality but what they want you to think is.

Most of the time, all it leads to is you liking an ex's new girlfriend's photo from her trip to Marbella ten years ago, never knowing if you've unliked it quick enough for it not to alert her. Or when you finally meet your crush and pretend that you didn't know they had two siblings, what their names were and about the family holiday to Padstow the previous year.

If you can't find them on social media, all that leaves is to think they must have a secret family or are a drug dealer, trying to not have any presence.

Then comes the Instagram stories – who's looking at them? Today was one of those days. After making my personal account private, no real surprises can come my way, but my business one obviously needs to be there for the world to see. You want people to see a part of you but not the half-naked beach photos that took most of the day to pose for.

'Soulmate', who's not reared his head in almost a year, has been looking. Naturally, my first reaction is that he must have changed; he now wants to live the life he promised me. But that's not the case, is it. What is simply someone being nosey turns my world upside down and causes me to think of every eventuality.

Maybe it was purely an accident, or most likely, he was drunk, and I still will not hear from him. It's little things like this that to one person can mean nothing, but to you means everything.

It's things like this that are causing you more harm than good, but for some reason, you can't stop. It's like an addiction that never really brings you happiness but helps you feel included.

I don't want to be known, but the fear of being unknown and invisible is worse.

Self-sabotage

I spend my time moaning about why I can't find the perfect man, or why people can't accept I haven't, yet am I really doing what's needed to change that? I've often been known to self-sabotage or to sabotage relationships for fear of speaking my truth. It somehow seems easier to force someone's hand into a break-up than to do the breaking up myself.

But what am I actually doing to change this? I meet up with men I know I have no future with, who actually lower my self-esteem and shy away from the ones that don't see me as some sort of project or admire me rather than feel I need their help.

I'm sure it's some sort of self-harm I do to myself. Without the option of taking drugs, I use situations that initially might make me feel high but afterwards have that come-down effect and just make me have regrets.

I remember once being so upset about a break-up I messaged someone to come round because I thought the only way I could stop crying was to have sex with someone else. Although I have been known to cry during sex, for other reasons entirely, I knew I wouldn't want to cry in front of this person. He was a one-pump chump, and for only a few minutes did I feel any sort of high.

After he left, I sat in the shower scrubbing myself clean and crying. Was it really worth those few escapism minutes?

When you've run out of ways to change the way you're feeling, men seem like the obvious option, but are the repercussions any less devastating? I'm left feeling worthless, and although I only wanted sex and sex alone, I'm left feeling used.

Am I just used to feeling this way and don't actually know whether I could cope with the alternative? There have been times when I have felt this happiness that I long for, only for it to explode into a million pieces or simply fade away. It's that uncomfortable comfort zone I can't seem to escape from.

The knot in my stomach and anxiety when I'm trying to fall asleep has somehow taken over me, and if I don't have reason to feel it, I don't know what to do.

What happens when we are fulfilled? Do we just end up boring? My friends often say they love hearing all my stories because they can live through me because their lives are so boring now. Why do we explain happiness as boring? Why do we identify drama with excitement? Are we not teaching each other that if you are truly happy and settled, you are now boring?

I saw a quote the other day that said, 'Rather than saying, "Sorry I'm late", say, "Thank you for waiting for me".' Do we need to stop glamourising drama and refer to that as boring and happiness as exciting?

We are so led by how the world refers to situations. It still pains me that there is never a Christmas advert of a group of friends just having a good time; it is always that family with children and a dog or a cat.

'Bad boys' are glamorised, and phrases like 'Treat them mean to keep them keen' exist. I mean, what the actual fuck!? Is it any wonder it's like the blind leading the blind?

Next time one of my happy coupled-up friends describes their lives as boring and say that mine is exciting, I'm going to correct them.

Being happy and fulfilled is exciting, being single is exciting, being unemployed can be exciting. Let's all stop using the word 'boring' to describe things.

The only thing I can describe as boring is having to sit through a gardening programme with my dad and sister, talking about different types of weeds and how to treat them.

But that is my boring, and what appears to be their exciting.

Single friends

The thing is, I don't have any truly single friends. The friends that aren't in relationships have children or live at least two hours away.

Where I live, I often say it's somewhere people come to settle or die. The vast majority of the population are either families or retired. The ones that are single are frequent pubgoers who get their kicks from blacking out on the weekend, only to start the countdown to Friday as soon as they open their eyes on Monday.

I love my friends, and it's taken me a long time to develop these connections. I find it far easier to find a new boyfriend than to find a new friend. But if I want this single path to succeed, I've got to put myself out there. Frankly, I feel more in need of a drink when doing this than I have on any date.

So, I've been asked out on a 'mate date', and anxiety is coursing through every vein in my body. I think without them having the option to at least be pleasured in the bedroom, I have to rely solely on my personality.

One of my close friends has always warned me off the idea of going out for a meal on a first date, something, to be honest, I've never had an issue with. As far as I'm concerned, a girl's got to eat! Then why am I feeling so stressed about going out for dinner with someone I know and who I have hung out with briefly on occasion?

I think the same ideas go through my head as when men

want to take me out. What do they want? Surely, they could hang out with someone better; is this some sort of prank? I know, seriously irrational thinking, but my thinking all the same.

I've had a lot of break-ups with friends over the years. A lot of the time, it was definitely my fault, but sometimes it wasn't. At times people can just drift apart, but I have had a few occasions where I have felt almost heartbroken and abandoned.

Everyone has at least heard of being ghosted by the opposite sex, but it can happen in friendships too, and this can be, at times, more painful. Romantic relationships have all sorts of reasons for ending, but friendships generally end because someone's stopped liking you as a person. I remember once a close friend saying I was too ill for her to see me. I appreciate now I was ill, but that rejection sticks with you.

I guess I feel the same about romantic relationships as I do about friendships: scared of getting hurt again, so best not to bother. But as a wise friend has just pointed out, being surrounded by just coupled-up friends with families is hardly going to help.

I need a balance; I need some single friends to stop me feeling like my life is escaping me. I need to remind myself that I am not Bridget Jones and have only been single for a matter of days, not months or years.

I have time, I just need to embrace the present and take some chances. Who knows, they might pay off.

Single and not ready to mingle

I'm now a few weeks into my new single status and feel I may have finally grown up. Usually, it takes me only a matter of weeks, sometimes days, to be drawn into the unknown world of internet dating. Maybe it is in part due to falling off the waggon, so to speak, with my most recent ex, or maybe I finally know what I need.

So, the first three weeks haven't been completely smooth or abstinent, but I have managed to stop myself from embarking on something new. I'm sure to most, this is easily done, but I seem to think men somehow justify my existence, so this is the most single I've been in a while.

My ploy so far has been to escape my usual surroundings to places where the dicksand can't get me. Last weekend I decided I was in need of some serious pampering, so went off to West Sussex with one of my go-to therapists and one part of my throuple. It's been months since she was off duty from playing mum and dutiful wife, something she seems to be doing in Crocs. Crocs have always been something of a faux pas in the fashion industry, but going through lockdown has caused many of us to break these all-important rules in favour of comfort. Added to this, she's only weeks away from giving birth and, I have to say, somehow pulls them off.

We arrive at what we hoped was pure luxury. She had been told by her mother that she thought she might like to dress up a bit, in other words, 'Don't wear the Crocs'. My mother had also insisted I take something smart for supper, something I, of course, took absolutely no notice of.

Before we had even entered the hotel, my friend faceplanted – was our trip to a spa actually going to end up in A&E!? I was never going to be able to see her again, I would be banned from the house, I would be taken off their Christmas list, and certainly wouldn't be invited to their next family holiday. All colour left my face, and I fussed round her, asking her a million questions very hysterically. She was in hysterics, but not crying. She was howling with laughter; she was more worried that someone might have seen her faceplant the tarmac at the entrance of this fancy hotel.

This is why we are friends. She has an air of calm around her; while I'm hysterical, she is cool as a cucumber, something she has painfully tried to teach me when it comes to men and life. Unfortunately, it has not rubbed off. Bump was all fine. The damage was only done to her knee, which was now bleeding all down her leg. So, it seems strappy sandals are not preferable over Crocs, especially when you are pregnant. Some things mothers don't get right.

We spent our time floating about in our robes and taking dips in different pools and jacuzzies. Apparently, when pregnant, there's nothing quite like being in water; the ache on your back suddenly goes, and what is now a heavy lump growing at the front of you now feels completely weightless. I, however, am not a water baby; my style of swimming is limited to the doggy paddle at best. Even this pregnant, she tried to teach me the art of swimming, but after panicking back into my doggy paddle, we decided laughing at my lack of grace was far easier than teaching me.

We'd booked the earliest slot for dinner; having not eaten for at least an hour, we were starving. The main hotel restaurant wasn't open due to something to do with Covid, so only the more relaxed cafe was on offer. It wasn't quite as smart as I'd imagined, not a single white tablecloth in sight; my mum would be horrified. Because of this, we both felt no obligation to take our robes off and constrict our bodies back into clothes, especially when about to embark on a three-course meal. Of course, we'd got it wrong, as the hostess explained disapprovingly that we must put some clothes on. I felt like I was a teenager again, being told off by my mother before I went to the nearby park to drink cider and smoke weed. After we arrived back rather sheepishly, she no doubt would have rather I'd stayed in my robe as opposed to my crop top and baggy trousers displaying my overly tattooed skin. At least I managed to avoid men this weekend, even if I didn't avoid embarrassment!

It seems my only way to get away from men was to completely leave the area and visit places that men were unlikely to visit. So far, that has been my mum's, a spa, and now back to my mum's. It would seem I may need to find other destinations or maybe just learn to have some self-control when home alone. Learn to deal with the loneliness and not be consumed by it. I can usually deal with weeknights, getting home from work and binge-watching the latest series I've become obsessed with. But there's something about Saturday nights that even as a non-drinker, I get the dreaded FOMO.

Most of the time, nothing is going on, and people are, in fact, doing nothing exciting and watching Saturday night tv with their respective partners. The idea of being home alone still feels uninviting and undoubtedly would end up being filled with ice creams and poor decisions. The loneliness would creep in, and I would text all the men I was trying not to text in hope that they would jump for joy at hearing from me.

I have to try and stick to this new way of life because I know in my gut it's the right decision. I try my best to live by the motto, 'What's meant to be, will be', and there is a lot of truth in that. I've gone from man to man, each slightly better than the last, but with no real idea what I want and need or if it's even possible.

Having come from divorced parents, it's something I want to try my best to avoid in my own life, something I'm sure they also tried. Without knowing myself single, can I really know what I want?

I don't just want to have the husband and the children, I want to be happy. I would choose happiness over having the supposed fairytale ending. I've spent so many years unhappy in relationships but trying to hold on in hope they might get better, or sometimes kidding myself that I was happy. A lot of the time, you can't see it until you're out of it, blinded by love or infatuation, just hoping and praying you don't have to go and sift through what Tinder has to offer.

I think, in part, the panic can come in when I look at where I live. It's renowned for being small, where everyone knows everyone, and if I know everyone, I don't think my lobster is here. Thankfully I'm taking time out, time off from the full-time job that is dating, and hopefully, now I will go into it when I'm ready and more sure of what I want rather than a slightly better version of the last.

Yes, I may have moments of doubt, loneliness, or wrong choices, but if I stay true to myself, hopefully, things will work out. People are quick to judge my need for keeping busy and taking myself off to be in my own version of male rehab. They say you need to get used to being on your own, but maybe I'm not ready to have that temptation. You have to make the right choices for you regardless of what other people agree with or understand. As long as you're being honest with yourself and others and try to be kind, the rest should fall into place.

My first baby love

I met my first real-life baby when I was twenty-one. Being the youngest, I never really came into contact with babies unless they were siblings of my friends, and frankly took no interest in them. I remember meeting her for the first time when she was only a week old. I would study her whole body, her tiny fingers and nails, her little chubby knees, her soft head. I was in awe; it seemed impossible to me that my friend had made her. It was an out-of-this-world experience. She fascinated me. She was well and truly my first baby love.

I would always make an effort to see my friend during her maternity leave, and of course, this included spending time with her baby. On more occasions than I would care to remember, I would get mistaken for her mother; this was no doubt due to the fact my friend had popped back into her size eight jeans, and I was going through an emotional eating stage. People would ask me how old she was and I would reply, 'Haven't got a clue,' like I'd stolen her from the local supermarket.

Saturday nights have changed somewhat over the years. They are no longer all about going out every weekend to restaurants and bars. This generally only happens once in a blue moon, in favour of having a grown-up pyjama party. If I can't turn up at your house in my pyjamas, you have to ask yourself, are we even friends? I don't want friends I feel I have to put on a show for. I want to be able to turn up with a conditioning treatment still in my hair, hoping I don't get stopped by the police whilst driving, and with my pyjamas on. She definitely qualifies as this sort of friend.

What is terrifying now, though, is my first baby love is now nine! I mean, how the fuck did that happen!? It seems only yesterday I was holding her and rocking her to sleep, and now she's doing cartwheels in the living room. It does seem like a pretty great age, though. She's in year five, so not in the anxiety-inducing year six, where you know it's only a matter of time before you have to go to 'big school'. You don't worry about putting your hand up in class and appearing over-eager or being in chess club, which was the case for me.

Speaking to her was pretty amazing; she told me how she had fourteen boyfriends, and they all fancied her, which was great, something I could never get away with now. She announced that she didn't think she'd ever wear makeup. We both, of course, agreed that she would never need to. She moaned that no matter how much she ate, she was still skinny. At this point, I had to remind myself she was just a child, and I couldn't be mad at her for her good genetics, although I told her to avoid saying that in front of other women. My friend and I told her that when she was being an annoying teenager, she would be sent to her Aunty Umbrella's (the name I'm now stuck with as she and her brother were never able to say my name). When she wore skirts that came round her chin, she would be sent to mine for a reality check; she innocently asked why she would ever wear short skirts like that. I think at this point, we felt that she'd have to learn more about that as she got older. I reminded her that all boys were very smelly, and she was always welcome to have a girlfriend instead.

At last, she told her mum, who is now a divorced single

mum of two, that she wanted her to have a sister for her. At which point, to save her mum's embarrassment, I announced I would have a little sister for her in a few years' time. How I am going to keep to this promise, I'm not quite sure, having neither a boyfriend nor the science to make sure I have a girl rather than a boy. So, my friend and I announced, we would get married, I would get a sperm donor, and we would all live happily ever after in adjoining houses. Something that seems more plausible at the moment than me finally finding the man of my dreams.

No doubt our upcoming nuptials will be the talk of the school, as we seem to forget how children are. When I was little, my parents' friend used to call me and my sisters his little sisters, and in turn, we would call him big brother. One day at the school gates, my mum was collared by a concerned parent. She told her that one of my sisters was going round saying a tall Ugandan man was her big brother. So, it seems only a matter of time before my friend is known as the lesbian mummy.

There are definitely worse future scenarios that could play out. As I left, she said, 'I love you, other mummy.' I finally felt some glimpse into what it would feel like to be someone's mum, and if I was only ever someone's other mummy, that would be just fine too.

Reasons not to date people

I'm an all-or-nothing kind of person; one is too many and a thousand never enough. I've been really good, by my standards at least, with keeping people at arm's length. With my quest to be alone, I've tried to keep away from temptation because when those feelings sneak in, I'm fucked.

Here I am fucked. I've gone from as cool as ice to hot like a furnace. People around me have wondered why I'm trying to keep men at a distance, and this is why: I go full crazy bitch. Added to this, those dreaded hormones have reared their ugly head, shouting, 'You need a baby' at every opportunity. So much so that I was even cooing over the babies in the baby shampoo advert yesterday. My younger self would be disgusted. Who is she? To be honest, I really don't know the answer to that.

If only people were to know what was going on in my head, they'd be sure to avoid me like the plague or get me hospitalised. So here I am, having fixated on my next victim, or old victim, one only a couple of weeks ago I was able to be nonchalant with. Now I seemed to have done a complete one-eighty and the crazy is seeping out! I'm constantly checking social media to see if he's posted anything, checking my stories to see if he's been watching. Even going as far as to click on his message to see if he's online; I've become pathetic. The funny part of this is he's completely clueless. He doesn't realise I'm fighting every bit of my being to message him. He thinks I'm still keeping him at arm's length because I want to be single.

How can you be broody and want to be single at the same time? Do I want to be single, or do I just not want to always be in the wrong relationship? I'm no longer sure I know what love is. The love I've thought I've felt has been so unbelievably unhealthy that there should be a rehab for it. It's not calm and comforting, it's anxiety-inducing. It's losing sleep and never knowing what's going to happen day to day, it's a constant state of panic. I seem to go for these men that provoke panic in me. I think I do this because I can deal with disasters; it's all I've ever known. If a nice guy came along and I bought into that, and it still ended badly, now that's a sure way of sending me over the edge.

People say how much they love the early parts of relationships, the excitement, the honeymoon period. Yes, of course, all the sex is great, but there tends to be a great deal of worrying and lack of sleep in those early days. I never know where I stand. Do they really like me? Oh fuck, I've got to get naked in front of this person! What if I fart!? My breath will smell in the morning, I'll look like shit.

How do you know if they're a nice guy and not simply a wolf in sheep's clothing? It has to be said I'm not the best judge of character. Can I have really done it again? It's now been over a week since I last saw the male in question. When I last saw him, things didn't quite go to plan. We've liked each other for a while, or so I thought. We were friends and helped each other through lockdown. I had made it pretty clear that I wanted to stay single for a while, but when I was with him, it was hard to stay strong.

Some people you meet and you have that instant attraction with – this wasn't the case with him. The Young

One is, of course, good-looking, but his personality was what got me hooked. We seemed to understand each other on a deeper level; he got my crazy, which is why I'm finding this apparent ghosting even more difficult. It's one thing to be ghosted by a guy you're dating, but something much more painful when you saw them as a friend. He knew I didn't want to be in a relationship yet has somehow managed to dangle the bait only to leave me alone and drowning.

When we were last together, we lay naked in each other's arms, discussing how many kids we wanted. Ok, I know my celibacy isn't quite going to plan! We had attempted to finally release the sexual tension that had been building between us, but it just wasn't meant to be. Maybe that was a sign. I will never understand how it is for a man to go through what they see as the embarrassment of not being able to perform. More often than not, I blame myself, thinking I'm not sexy enough, I'm doing something wrong, but I tried not to make this about me and comfort him instead. The days that followed, I tried to send supporting messages and offered to go and see him, which all seemed to fail. As the week went on with little contact, my crazy reared its ugly head. Most women may like to keep their cards closer to their chest, but I'm painfully honest, and I knew he'd understand.

I messaged him again, asking him if he was free that evening, yet again I received a pie to the face. Last week he seemed to do anything possible to see me, now it seems he was avoiding me like I was a crazy ex-girlfriend. He said he'd let me know when he was free, and being the people pleaser I am, I said of course, that was fine. But here I am, nearly a week on from that, and not even a message to say he's really busy or needs some space. Someone I valued so much in my life now doesn't seem to care at all.

You don't always have to have sex to be intimate. For me, intimacy is the drug, and it's the drug that all the dealers seem to have run out of. It was like when I would ring my dealer to score, and he'd tell me he was at one part of town. I spent God knows how long walking there, no distance too far, only on arriving for him to tell me he was now where I had started, and so the chase would go on and the need would get stronger.

So, when I tell people I need to be alone, this is the reason. I've gone from feeling empowered in my new single status to having a taste of that addictive drug, only to be left short. Maybe this was not meant to be my happily ever after, but these men feel like pushers, and I'm back in the gutter trying to work out how the fuck I got back here.

A wise friend, who of course doesn't take her own advice, because none of us do, said...

'Trust in the process; this door may have closed only for the right one to open.'

If only it were that easy.

Power

I lay on the gym mat doing some sort of exercise instructed to me, with an older, good-looking guy exercising on a mat a meter away from me and realised this is the most intimate I'm going to be with a man in a while. The panic hit me, and honestly, I could have cried right there and then. In my life, I've always had a backup, someone on the cards, someone I could call up in desperation. I either don't have that, or I've finally found some self-worth.

It's amazing how one knock in my romantic rollercoaster can cripple me. Suddenly I'm more unattractive, fatter, less funny, and older than I was only yesterday. A man's validation becomes the utmost important thing, and yet again, I lose myself in the process.

But I am a powerful, strong, beautiful, badass woman. Even though I cringe as I write that. But I am, and I do not need a man to make me feel worthy of living. Things have changed for women for a reason, and here I am moping about waiting for any available – well, mostly unavailable – man to give me a pat on the back and say, 'You're good enough.' When did I stop doing this for myself? Have I ever done this for myself? Do they live to be accepted by us? I highly doubt it.

I spent most of yesterday crying yet again about another failed romance that didn't even make it past the start line. I cried in the work cafe, in the toilet on the phone to my friend, to another friend at work, but, worst of all, I cried to the male in question. I gave him my power, I gave him my self-worth, and he managed to crumple it in an instant. It has to be said that when people say not to react straight away, there's a reason for it. Maybe I would have reacted differently to the situation if I hadn't already dealt with an ex that day or the fact I hadn't slept because I was stressed by the mess the whole world's in at the moment.

I have fought so hard to be the woman I've become and have had to use every fibre in my being not to fall apart on numerous occasions, yet I happily give myself to the nearest person that blinks at me. Less than forty-eight hours later, I've created a playlist with only the best empowering songs I can find, absolutely no love songs in sight. I am dusting myself off yet again and putting my positive pants on. Yes, I feel embarrassed and vulnerable, but I also feel powerful. I own my life and only I can change it.

I did like this person, but as usual, I chose to ignore that he didn't meet some of my critical needs. He probably drinks more than I would like, has been known to not only enjoy rich-man-candy but also deal it, but most importantly, hasn't been able to communicate his feelings.

I'm currently reading a book called Attached, which is a real eye-opener. There are apparently three different types of attachment style: secure attached, anxious attached and avoidant attached. I seem to be one of the unlucky few that falls into both anxious attached and avoidant attached. The ideal would be to find someone that is secure attached, but as the book goes on to explain, there are significantly fewer of these in the dating pool. Why? They generally get into and stay in relationships. So basically, what we're left with isn't great. But learning about myself and why I'm prone to do the things I do is beyond helpful. It recommends that if you are anxious attached, you should date numerous people at a time. For me, this feels so unbelievably unnatural as a serial relationshipper. But there is method in the madness! If you only date one person, it is very easy, as I have done countless times before, to develop feelings for people that categorically do not meet your needs. If you have an array of different people, you are more likely to not get attached to one person and, well, shop around without feeling pressure to make a decision. Genius!

Another way I've heard to keep my power is not to put out! A few friends have asked me recently how quickly I sleep with people, and I felt like I was back in the Middle Ages about to be condemned for fornicating with men. I've spent a long time wanting to be equal to a man and be allowed to sleep with whoever I want, whenever I want, without ever asking myself, 'Is it actually right for me?' By the looks of it, it definitely is not. It's a well-known fact that women's bodies have different reactions to men's when you have sex. Women release oxytocin when having sex; this is a hormone linked to 'positive social functioning and is associated with bonding, trust and loyalty', according to Dr. Sal Raichbach, a psychologist and licensed clinical social worker. This isn't all women. I know many that don't seem to have this issue, but I do. So, it would seem that by trying to have this carefree bravado, I am setting myself up for a fall.

It's not until you begin to learn about all these things that you can better understand what YOU really need. Everyone is different. Some of my girlfriends have slept with people without getting attached. Some haven't slept with anyone for months and are not bothered, and don't even masturbate. Some love slow tantric sex, while others like wearing nipple clamps and being beaten for kicks. The possibilities are endless. It seems once you can identify who you are and what you want and need, therein lies your power. So here's my attempt...

- I am anxious attached, with a bit of avoidant attached thrown in for good measure.

- I need constant reassuring and abundance of affection.

- I also want my own space and do not want to be controlled or gushy public displays of affection.

- I like doing things with a partner, but my friends are my world.

- If I have sex with you, I will probably develop strong feelings for you even if you are completely wrong for me.

- I cannot have one-night stands successfully.

- I should date numerous people instead of putting all my eggs in one basket.

- I should wait longer before jumping into bed with someone; I have a vibrator – use it.

- I do not want to be a mother figure, I want to be an equal.

- I don't find it attractive when men can't use a washing machine.

- If you rely on me too much, I will distance myself.

- If you distance yourself, I will become more needy.

- I want the romantic gestures.

- I don't want to have to constantly reassure someone that I like them.

I'm not sure if this man exists, but at least I know what my triggers are. The more we learn to understand ourselves, love ourselves, believe we are amazing people worthy of love, the more likely we are to attract the right type of mate. Or here's hoping – I am by no means an expert! But I finally, for this moment at least, have my power.

The pros and cons of living alone

Pros

- The whole bed to yourself
- Everything being where you left it
- Being able to eat ice cream for dinner without judgement
- Wearing granny pants without judgement
- Watching whatever you want on tv
- Knowing when you've run out of toilet roll
- Your expensive products not being used by anyone else
- Not having to share food
- Not being kicked in bed
- Not being woken up by snoring
- Being able to wear mouth guard, silk hat and eye mask to bed without judgement
- Not being woken up by other people's alarms
- Choosing own music to play loudly when getting ready
- Not having to be quiet when waking up early to go to the gym
- Not being expected to make anyone a coffee when you make yourself one

- Farting, burping and going to the toilet without running the tap or turning up the tv
- Being able to masturbate whenever you want without damaging anyone's ego
- Not having to talk after a long day of talking at work

Cons

- No one to cuddle in bed
- No one to cook for, or cook for you
- No one else buying toilet roll
- Having to sort out all bills
- Fixing the occasional pipe
- Not always knowing how to fix things
- Not being made coffee
- No one else doing the washing up
- No one else doing the food shopping
- Having to ring tradesmen
- Dealing with tradesmen who are constantly looking for 'the man of the house' to talk to
- No one pulling you out of your dark mood
- Having to look after yourself when you're ill
- No possibility of sex every night unless you have a reliable booty call
- No one to moan to about a long day at work

- The house being dark when you get in
- Being the one that fights off burglars

There are many pros and cons, but it's not guaranteed that whoever you have living with you eliminates those cons or doesn't add to them. They still might use the last of the loo roll and not replace it. They might not know how to fix things and sometimes rely on you to sort shit out. At the moment, the pros far outweigh the cons. I have friends that can stay in my bed and I can spoon, and they might even be able to work out why all my lights have tripped. The more I am alone, the more I can deal with the things that I never thought I'd be able to deal with. The more I've been in relationships, the more I've re-alised they often can't deal with any of those things either. We can't be in relationships in hope that the 'blue jobs' will be done, in the same way I would hate a man to think by being with me, the 'pink jobs' will be done for him.

I now have a timer that switches my lamp on when it gets dark, so I don't get back to a dark home. I've got a cleaner, well, because I can, and would far rather eat beans on toast all week so I can afford one. I have friends that will come and help me when there's a leak or I need to put a picture up. One friend even turned up at my house at 6.30 am because my front door had jammed shut and I couldn't get out.

My friends are the most amazing people, each with their own skill set. I don't need the figure of a man in my life to survive at life. I just need to have faith that I can do both 'pink' and 'blue' jobs, or the 'purple' jobs as I now call them.

My great loves

'Maybe our girlfriends are our soulmates and guys are just people we have fun with.'

Carrie Bradshaw

It wasn't until my late twenties that I realised what true friendship was. I had spent my earlier years relying on boyfriends to be everything I needed, too scared to make female friends and face rejection. The limited friends were primarily male, which always led to one of us getting our feelings hurt. It's that old debate – can the opposite sex really just be friends? For me, it's a resounding NO.

I of course had girlfriends, but it wasn't until the year I broke up with my long-term boyfriend, Prince Charming, that I felt completely loved and accepted by these women. This was by no means to do with them as people, only my own insecurities. I would describe myself as more of a jealous friend than I am partner; luckily, these women have gotten used to my green-eyed monster and accept me as I am.

One of my major insecurities when it comes to friends is introducing them, so I generally don't. I've had these friends for years and some have never met, only heard of each other. It's what I'm sure most women might feel when introducing their partner to one of their hot friends. I worry that they will no doubt like each other more than they like me because, let's face it, my friends are badass, and well, I'm mostly just ass.

I wonder if I will ever find a man I have more fun with than my girlfriends. Someone that accepts me more than they do and has my back no matter what. We're told that everyone has a soulmate, that someone is waiting to find us. Firstly, who the fuck are these people that release this sort of information? And how do they know?

But enough about fucking men – that's not what this chapter is about! No, my great loves are all in female form, a lot more reliable and a lot less disappointing!

I think I've found my soulmates – yes, mates – and they are my girlfriends. They were sent to me when I needed them the most, maybe because I needed them. That's my lot of luck in life, and to be honest, if it is, I will die a happy woman.

Growing up, I didn't have this advantage; I was painfully shy and struggled to build lasting relationships. The only relationships that seemed to last were those with men, and I'm still convinced that's mainly been due to the fact we've been bonded by sex.

With friends, there is no sex, nothing to make us stay if we find them to be controlling, possessive and toxic. They don't live in your house, they don't have possessions left at yours, and if someone isn't adding to your life, it is a lot easier to get rid. There have been such friends in my life, and at a time, I was that friend. Thankfully I'm a very different person now and haven't been ghosted in that way for many years.

I find it almost magical that such amazing, strong women have entered my life just when I've needed them. They have, in fact, helped mould the woman I am today. With gentle guidance and a fair bit of frustration, they have helped me get through many traumas in my life, both real and the ones completely fabricated in my head.

The thing about having different friends is it's a lot more acceptable than having lots of different boyfriends, and frankly, one man in my life is more than enough. Some people might be able to be in a non-monogamous relationship, seeing one for good sex, and another for great adventure, but that isn't for me. However, I can have the same benefits with my friends.

There are friends I can go dancing with until the early hours, only to be left pulling their pants up in the toilet or holding their hair back while they throw up. I have friends I can be silly with, belly laugh with, and who always seem to be able to comfort me when I'm down. I have friends I can go and walk twenty miles with on a Sunday and see a sunrise and realise there is no place I would rather be in that moment.

I've had to learn over the years that one person cannot fulfil all your wants and needs, and a lot of them you have to do for yourself. But if you're willing to put work into these friendships and nurture them the same you would a man, you might just find those soulmates that they speak about.

To the loves of my life, I will be eternally grateful for having you around.

Modern-day flirting

When I was little, if a boy was horrible in the school playground, I was told, 'It's because he likes you.' We are brought up thinking that if someone is mean to you, it's because they like you. This is a pretty fucked-up way of looking at things. If that is the case, I'm pretty sure every boy and girl at my school fancied me. The one that once hit me with a branch was no doubt head over heels in love with me.

This has been ingrained in us from such a tender age, and probably where the whole idea of 'treat them mean to keep them keen' came from. We are told that people that are mean to us fancy us, so is it any wonder when people ignore us, ghost us, and are downright abusive to us, we see this as love!? No wonder I haven't found a nice man to marry because I keep chasing the ones that are pricks.

Now as I'm slightly older, being mean to me initially doesn't always work. However, I'm not saying it never does. Unless people are drunk, it's very rare they flirt in the broad light of day – how do you even do that anyway? With dating apps to hide behind, the internet has become the home to where you can flirt without the embarrassment of getting publicly pied in the face. It's not only dating apps that give you this opportunity though. Any social media acts as a platform for you to 'flirt' under some ridiculous invisibility blanket, even though you're not invisible, and could quite easily bump into them when you're next buying Femfresh in your local supermarket.

My translation of social media:

Friend request/follow request:

- They were at primary school with you
- You are their third cousin twice removed
- You have the same surname
- They're going out with your ex
- They think you're hot
- You slept with them once
- They're a friend of a friend
- They're nosey
- They want to sleep with you
- An old friend that wants to see how fucked up you are now
- They've seen you in the gym
- You've met them at work
- They're the husband of a client
- Might be interested in your work, but more than likely, one of the above
- They're an ex of an ex (ready to do some voodoo doll shit)
- They've seen you out and about but never spoken to you, and never will

I do my best not to accept most of the people listed above – well, unless they're hot and I want to sleep with them (relatives obviously not included).

Likes/Loves and all the other reactions:

- They like the photo (obvious, I know)
- They're one of your squad
- They're in your family
- They fancy you
- They want to fuck you (definitely if it's an old photo)
- It's got your dog in it
- It's got one of your friends' babies in it
- An inspirational quote
- You're in a bikini or somewhere exotic

Stories – who's snooping:

- Bored people
- Your ex
- Your ex's girlfriend
- They fancy you
- They want to fuck you
- Nosey people
- Your squad
- Your family
- They want you to know they're looking (an ex, or a possible soon-to-be ex)

Now obviously, this is just my interpretation, and if they're hot and not my ex, I generally read into everything and think they must fancy me. This is obviously with the help of my girl squad, who encourage my craziness while looking them up on Facebook and telling me, 'He's got a really kind face in that wedding he went to in 2014.' We're all guilty of it. We stalk our prey, trying to work out if they're a douchebag or not, nine times out of ten painting them out to be an idyllic, caring, Jude Law in *The Holiday* type.

I get so drawn into it. The other day, I was feeling a bit down after going to London for my sister's boyfriend's birthday. They are so lovely together it makes me want to vomit in my mouth, but I adore them both, so I put up with it. We were out with some of his football team, one of whom I thought seemed quite nice. My sister's boyfriend started trying to play Cilla Black, only for me to realise that not only was he twenty-four – not great when I'm currently having a meltdown about being old – but he also loves a bit of rich-man-candy. Is there anyone out there that doesn't!? So, I'm stalking another potential prey on Instagram. There's a guy that lives round the corner from me that is super-hot, but have I ever spoken to him? No! Would I ever start a conversation with him? No! But a cheeky follow on Instagram? Why not!

And so, it starts, the painful waiting. After I followed him, to be honest, I forgot about it. The following day I woke to a follow back! Jackpot! Then about five minutes later, he liked a picture I posted about a month ago of me and my dog. So, the follow back could have been innocent, but liking an old photo, in my translation, he definitely wants a shag. So, what do I do next? It's like a game of chess! I scroll through his feed to realise the only picture of him is the first photo he ever posted – way too creepy to like that. The rest were work-related, so what now? After waiting at least twenty-four hours, I decide to like a picture of a flower he posted. A fucking flower! What was I doing!? And so, the slow, agonising chess game continues.

'Now what?' you ask yourself. Well, let's post a story, even though you have nothing to post but want to see if they're snooping. My morning coffee, I'm such a melt. Then for the remainder of the day, check who's looked at your story at every opportunity to see if he's looked at it. By this point, in my head, I have decided he's not a frequent Instagrammer like myself. Only work-related pictures and no stories to stalk, so my hope is dwindling, especially as it's nearly the end of the day and he's not looked at my super interesting story of my morning coffee with the caption, 'Perfect start to my week'. I'm so cringe!

Alas, it's now 9 pm, and finally, he's looked at my super boring coffee! But now what? By following him, I've basically said, 'Hi'. In turn, he's said, 'Hi, I might fancy you, or want to fuck you, or just think your dog's cute.' I've then responded by saying, 'I like that flower, I fancy you, and I might want to fuck you too.' But in reality, no words have been exchanged. I'm already exhausted. Now it's just a waiting game – who is going to give in and make the first move? Or is it just going to be another person I follow that I think is hot, and if I see in the street will no doubt ignore because I haven't got my invisibility blanket with me?

And people wonder why I'm single.

Internet dating, part two

The mongrel is back! It seems social media flirting is too slow, so I have decided to have another flutter. It seems being COMPLETELY single was too much for me to handle. For the sake of the poor unsuspecting men that have to suffer my conversation skills, I hope I won't be about long. But reading my conversations, I would suspect I will be on the market longer than any of us would like.

Technology can be amazing. I'm able to scroll through photos I sent my friends long ago. I often send my friends all conversations I have with possible suitors, or their photos, etc.

> *'Your collective dating record reads like a who's who of human crap.'*
>
> *Phoebe Buffay*

And one day, I stumbled across one such conversation. I remember at the time thinking this guy was really rude. Coming across it again, I was mortified by what I saw. Was I, in fact, the dumb person with no chat that I so often ridicule?

It turns out that I am.

Now I don't know if I had overdosed on talking to people, or I need glasses, or I am a little bit dyslexic. (I just had to say that word into my phone to spell it – surely, given the diagnosis, it should be easier to spell!)

Anyway, poor unsuspecting Jack did come across someone who read CHEF every time he wrote CHIEF. He told me how he was a firefighter training to be a chief. I replied by saying how I love a man that can cook, and when he tried to correct me, I said, 'Oh, are you training to be a sous chef then?' After maybe the fourth or fifth comment I made about him being a chef, he eventually lost his temper and replied in only capitals trying to explain the difference between a chief and a chef... I still didn't get it.

I mean, seriously! Thank God, I don't see this guy wandering the streets because no doubt I would ask how his cheffing is going.

I now am even more convinced that if I am to take to this internet dating saga again that my friends should take it over for me. Maybe they would stop feeling like their lives are boring, and I could stop dying inside.

Who knows, this guy could have been 'the one' if I could only tell the difference between a CHIEF and a CHEF. As the kids say today, FML.

Earth man

It's now Friday evening, and I have technically the second date with Social Media Flirting Guy. He was on Bumble, and it appears this is a slightly easier way to connect than going backwards and forwards liking each other's pictures! I've got to be honest, I wasn't that excited. He seemed nice, but I don't like nice, so was left feeling indifferent to our first meeting. Nonetheless, I wanted to have an open mind and just give things a go. After feeling pretty calm, I suddenly turned into a woman possessed. My bedroom floor now resembles that of a messy child with clothes thrown everywhere.

I FaceTimed my friend, trying on different outfits, before hanging up on her pre-breakdown. Usually, it takes me about half an hour to get ready. I'm not one for spending hours preening, especially when sex was off the table. I eventually managed to pull myself together and pick an outfit before walking to meet him.

Then the worst possible thing happened: I actually liked him. With sex off my radar (for now) I actually had to hold a conversation, no flirting, no innuendos, just our interests and our lives. How could I have been so indifferent? Should I have really been giving other people a chance previously that I'd dismissed?

We went for a Thai, and I chose noodles. Never again. I had completely overlooked the fact I would actually have to eat them without looking more tramp than lady. He obviously saw I was struggling too and tried to comfort me, saying he felt like he'd forgotten how to use cutlery. He put me at ease, and we both managed to laugh at my faux pas. I went to the loo, partly because I needed it, partly to flash the more sexy side of my outfit, and on my return, realised he'd paid. A gentleman at last!

He happens to live round the corner from me, so we walked home together, and he invited me in for tea. This appeared to be a civilised invitation and not code for a fuck. He lit the fire and we continued to chat until nearly midnight. At one point, I remember complimenting him on the useful space under his stairs, more proof that I definitely don't need alcohol and have reached some weird middle age where you say that sort of thing.

We hugged goodbye, and I felt a slight awkwardness between us – should we kiss? We didn't, and I went home and cuddled my dog for half an hour, feeling pleased I'd given him a chance and behaved like a proper adult and not stripped off on the first date.

Welcoming back my crazy bitch head... the following morning, I message him, thanking him for a lovely evening, saying I hope the grouting on the tiles went OK today (he's renovating his house). He replied, saying thanks, you too, and he will let me know how it goes. As I'm trying to be more chilled, I didn't reply to his message. It didn't need replying to, and I need to stop worrying about offending people by not replying when they probably don't expect one. Nearly forty-eight hours later and I've heard nothing. Last week when he took a couple of days to message me or even read my message and took the whole day to reply, I was unfazed.

But now I like him. So, does this mean men only get the cool, calm and collected version of me if I don't like them?

And they get the crazy bitch if I do? Fuck, I feel sorry for these men.

Fast forward a few days, and finally, I'm getting a bit of conversation out of him, not much, but enough. We arrange to meet on Sunday and go for a dog walk. He's not been overly forthcoming, so I try my best to act chilled and not arrange too much other than the walk, and try and just go with the flow. The dog walk was nice, and again we bounced off each other, so we agreed to go back to his and order some food. The chemistry seemed to be tingling between us; I was definitely going to get a kiss tonight.

As we ate dinner, he suggested watching a film and having a snuggle. He was sweet, no obvious flirting, but maybe this is what nice guys are like.

Snuggling on the sofa, I wasn't sure how much longer I could take it. Finally, the film came to an end and the long-awaited kiss happened, opened-mouthed and slobbery. Maybe he was nervous, so I tried to continue, and there I was, straddling him like a crazed animal, feeling like I was a teenager who had had one too many lines of coke. Not a lot of dialogue was exchanged, and before I knew it, I was naked in his bed, waiting for the inevitable to happen.

How the fuck did it go from a kiss to that in a matter of minutes? No flirting, no real build-up, just bang. The worst part, the bang wasn't even worth it. It was a temporary fix for a much deeper-rooted problem. I was so pissed off at myself, ashamed and full of regret. I thought those feelings didn't happen once you stopped drinking and taking drugs. I couldn't even bring myself to tell my friends until weeks later, having yet again tried to get over someone by getting under someone else.

But alas, I continued to kid myself that I hadn't just slept with someone to fill the void building inside me. I went back round his a few days later, convincing myself that you need to get to know someone better for the fireworks to be there. We decided to watch a film, and he proceeded to fall ASLEEP on me. Now I'm no dating guru, but to fall asleep on someone that you've only met three times seemed a little bit comfortable for me. So, you've seen my vagina and now you can kick back and stop making any effort? I didn't even get a happy ending at the end of the night.

I left his place feeling somewhat frustrated and flabbergasted. At least I knew there was a happy ending waiting for me at home, and the only thing I'd allow to fall asleep on me was my dog.

Shockingly the conversation dwindled off more, and I have to say I was relieved. I eventually got a message saying, in a nutshell, 'It's me and not you', explaining his life was too chaotic to date but he'd really like to stay friends.

However, there is a silver lining to this cloud: I managed to sleep with someone without falling in love with them. At this moment in time, I'm clinging on to any positivity I can get.

The journey and not the destination

Right now, I have no idea where 'the destination' is, so the obvious answer would to be at least try and enjoy the journey. I've yet again decided the dating world is not for me. The problem with self-discovery is that once you see something, you can't unsee it.

I've not been truly single – no dating, no sex, no chatting to anyone – for fifteen years. After my latest dating disaster and feeling like I couldn't be bothered to speak to anyone, added to which there was a second lockdown, I decided it was about time for a proper dicktox. But where does that leave me? It appears when you constantly get under someone to get over someone, you're never really over a lot of those people. Well, in my case, anyway.

I now appear to be grieving every relationship I've had in the past fifteen years. Each day it seems a new person comes into my mind and sadness sweeps over me. Were they all bad? Maybe I should just message them, seeing where their head's at.

My first sexual encounter was with a guy a couple of years older than me. He was in a heavy metal band, so obviously super cool. When he broke up with me, my world imploded, and I would cry into the unicorn toy he'd bought me for Valentine's Day that he actually gave me the night we broke up. I remember sobbing on him, only to try to pretend it wasn't about him and claim I didn't think my dad loved me. At this point, I don't know who I feel more sorry for, him or me.

Fast forward sixteen years, and of course, we follow each other on social media. In my head, I'm thinking, wouldn't that be a great story to tell the grandkids, separated for sixteen years and now look at us! We exchanged a few messages, nothing particularly inappropriate, then I got nothing. A few days later, he'd put up on his story a picture of him and a baby, 'Today I became a father.' Queue breakdown.

Yet again, I've fallen into the trap of romanticising an imaginary relationship. Another of my exes appears to have his life together and has even become a father! Here I am, too lazy and scared to find someone new, so going through my black book of exes and wondering why I'm coming up short.

The thought has even crossed my mind to hook back up with Weekend Offender after he messaged the other day claiming he's yet again broken up with his girlfriend and to let me know when I want to get married. So desperate am I to have that family that appears on the outside to be all sunshine and flowers that I'm willing to settle for something that is a dormant volcano ready to erupt. Someone call the asylum because it appears I need to be locked away; apparently, locked down isn't enough.

What has this taught me, though, the real nitty gritty of it? I don't love and accept myself. It pains me to write that, but I've spent years seeking men's validation to tell me, 'I love you, just as you are' like Mark Darcy did to Bridget Jones.

I spend my days thinking of stories I can put up on Instagram to get a reaction from men, but there's only so much to put up in this current climate. A picture of my dog, or me and my dog, or food – it's hardly 'come to bed' eyes. And why do I do this? To yet again get some recognition and validation from the opposite sex.

So here I am playing Alanis Morrissette a little too loudly, trying to evoke some more of the tears that I always seem to shed on my friends at the drop of a hat, but nothing. I feel like I'm going through yet another break-up when a relationship hadn't even started, but in my head, it had. The Young One was a nonstarter, apparently not to be. Surely there are only so many times you can blame timing before you accept it was never meant to be. Unfortunately, the pain of what could've been still lives on, and it's haunting me.

I've now dwelled on this for long enough, and frankly, it's getting a bit pathetic. I'm a thirty-year-old woman with a mortgage and a dog, crying over someone that clearly doesn't care for me. But unfortunately, there is no quick fix; there is no drug that will take the sadness away. No amount of men I sleep with will get me over this, or any of the ones that came before him.

This is the journey, I've realised, learning to love and accept me for me. Maybe if I hadn't continuously slept with other people or gotten into new relationships, I wouldn't be mourning the loves of my life all at once. It's like a punch to the stomach that I wasn't expecting, and it seems to have winded me beyond belief. One day I'm upset about one of my exes, only to be upset over another the next day. So, it pains me to say this, but getting under to get over does NOT work. It is a temporary fix for a bigger problem.

So here I am in my fourth decade, trying to work out how to get over someone for the first time. Thankfully I'm better equipped than I was all those years before. I'm no longer addicted to drugs, which does little for your social life. Nor am I in a relationship that I'm putting before my friends. I have such beautiful, inspiring women in my life today that no man could ever measure up to.

When I fall apart, which is often, they are there to pick me up. They fully accept me for the person I am. They love me, just as I am. They are Mark Darcy multiplied and in female form.

If this rollercoaster of a journey I find myself on has taught me anything, it's that your friends are your everything. They have been brought to you when you've needed them the most. They have wiped away your tears, brought homemade food in for you to eat when you have no appetite. They are the ones that don't go, and they are the ones that will be by your side forever.

To those I've loved before

*'She loves deeply regardless of the love she
gets in return, and it's both her biggest strength
and her biggest weakness.'*

N.R Hart

When I love, I love with every bit of my being; those I
have loved will know this. There have been many men
along the way that I have given this love to freely, without
asking for much in return. To me, that love never really
goes. I will always hold them in a part of my heart even
though it's more than likely I can no longer have them in
my life.

It's true for me that these men become my world, my
reason for being, and more times than not, I lose myself
completely. I'm a die-hard romantic that grew up watching
films like *Romeo and Juliet*, thinking that if you weren't
willing to commit suicide for someone, was it even love?

Last night I lay in bed trying to get myself to sleep the
only way I know how; a bit of self-love is usually the
answer. I lay there thinking of loves gone by, trying to
reach that ecstasy that I used to feel, only to feel tears
falling down my face once I'd reached it.

The loves I've felt have been far from healthy, and I know
that deep in my heart, but I'm not willing to settle for
mediocre. The more I love someone, the better the sex is,
or so I've found. You share a part of you that's precious, a
part that's not shared with anyone that you happen to roll

around with.

I've learnt a lot from these men, and it's not been all bad. Most men have loved me entirely back, although many have taken me for granted whilst in a relationship with me, only to realise this when I finally start to put my sanity first. You can only give so much before your soul is crushed, and ultimately, you have to choose yourself, no matter how much you love them.

It's been a slow, painful process, but I'm getting better at this as the years go on, and with the right support around me. This, unfortunately, doesn't mean they ever leave me completely. I don't wish for bad things to happen to any of my exes. The other day a mutual friend informed me that one of my exes 'hadn't changed', as he put it, and he and his girlfriend were having problems. In the past, I may have revelled in this, but today, I just feel sad. The reason people act badly towards you more often than not is a reflection on how they see themselves. Being my own worst enemy, I know first-hand what a painful place that is to be, and don't wish that on anyone.

Today I am single, in every sense of the word. So hopefully, with a bit of practice, I'll be able to use that love I so freely give to men and give it to myself. If I could give just an ounce of that to myself, maybe I would start to realise how much I deserve.

THIS IS 31

New year, old me

It has to be said my New Year's Eve was, by far, not my worst. Having spent previous New Year's in A&E, crying on the pavement, arguing with whichever boyfriend I was with, or in blackout so I missed the celebrations entirely. However, it was not what I had planned for my first one single in more than a decade.

As my bubble and I (if you've lived through 2020, you now know what a 'bubble' is) watched Big Ben chime midnight with not so much as a small crowd present, a sudden sadness swept over me. I had planned for my first Christmas and New Year single to be that of massive celebrations. I myself wasn't even convinced I'd make it. Instead, I've spent the evening with my friend in our pyjamas playing games and eating too much food.

If Covid has highlighted anything to me, it has been the importance of families. However much I usually opt out of Christmas, this year, I'd decided not to – made more important by the news of my dear grandpa's passing only weeks before. But it wasn't to be, the country divided by a new tier system locking most of them down without any chance of us seeing each other.

So, of course, I look around me for comfort and escape and am greeted by my friends, who all have their own respective families, whether that's the whole package or just their children. I felt so alone.

I walked to the cathedral the day after hearing the news

about my grandpa to light a candle for him, knowing he'd approve. I'm not sure when the last time I set foot in a church was, but I fear it was three years earlier with him in Spain. Everywhere I walked, there were families and couples, ever reminding me that I was in this alone. I walked through the lit city with tears running down my face, for my grandpa and for myself.

It's amazing how grief could make me feel. The sudden urge to find my match and procreate became intoxicating. The need for a man's arms wrapped round me, comforting me, something no matter how hard my girlfriends tried, just didn't match up.

There I was at midnight, on New Year's Eve, with the same longing. Someone to kiss at midnight and hold me and tell me that everything was going to be OK. What is it in me that needs this to be a man? Or is it my biological clock slowly ticking inside me, which appears to be getting louder every day?

As in a lot of cases, a few flames gone by appeared after hearing of my sad news. One in particular that, unfortunately, I don't appear to be able to remove from under my skin. The one that seems almost the most bizarre, when we were never even anything to get over.

I often romanticise situations in my head, I'm fully aware of that. I paint a picture of something that is and was never really there. But I don't know how to stop it. Can you really love someone you've never been with, or even get over someone for that matter? Have I, in fact, watched too much Friends and have painted it as Ross and Rachel's on-again-off-again relationship that turns out all right in the end?

It's true I never thought in a million years I'd be the single one out of all my friends. Having stuck with relationships far longer than I should have done, I believed my stubbornness to the cause would prevail. But here I am, the only one that is truly alone, and with every new engagement, new date, and new baby, I stand here trying to smile with encouragement when inside, I feel like I'm falling apart.

Here's hoping that not being married off yet simply means I miss out on my first divorce.

I'm doing this for my grandpa, the man who didn't believe in divorce. Or at least that's what I'm going to tell myself.

P.H.P.

1923-2020

Fear

On the other side of fear lies freedom. I appear to have found myself in a place I've never been before. Throughout most of my life, when it came to relationships, I was carefree and committed without any hesitation. I jumped in with both feet, often prematurely.

I now find myself completely fearful of the prospect of being in a committed relationship. Before, I would often concentrate on all the positives, and now only the negatives are highlighted. It appears when you've been hurt one too many times, you build a wall that even the most adventurous explorer can't climb.

A close friend is having therapy and was asked to describe their wall that's holding them back. Her wall was almost idyllic; it was that of a fortress, one I could imagine being in *Game of Thrones*. Mine, on the other hand, was covered in barbed wire, had spikes sticking out of it, with layers of concrete before reaching the original brick wall. Added to which it was beneath a dark cloud. Not one I would want to try and climb, but one I must in order to reach the freedom.

I found myself in tears this morning, having arranged a date with someone I'm pretty sure I like, only to suddenly not want him anywhere near me after overthinking the whole situation. Nothing had changed; he'd done nothing wrong, yet I had to catastrophise the whole situation. He had got back in touch with me around the time my grandpa died, and it's fair to say I was feeling alone and pretty vulnerable. He offered friendship when I said that's all I wanted, but yet again, is that just a man's kryptonite? After a few weeks of me putting my boundaries up, I finally broke and allowed it to become more. Is this just more proof you can't be friends with someone you slept with?

Wishing to have that idyllic family one day, I must first deal with the fears that have been etched on me like tattoos. As you get older, it appears finding that special someone comes with its own difficulties. Where I was once carefree, I now am terrified. Hoping that I never again have to feel the pain of heartbreak, but knowing it is probably inevitable.

I loved the new self I had found since breaking up with Prince Charming, and ultimately Soulmate as well. I felt empowered, strong, and independent, but it appeared it was always masking the trauma it had caused.

It dawned on me I had not been openly (on social media) in a relationship since Prince Charming. I feel anxious going on a date or being seen with a male where I live, in fear I will be the subject of people's gossip. It appears I have been masking my newfound strength with weakness. I long to be completely true to myself and not worry about what people think.

I often think about what it must be like for people who don't think as much as I do. How peaceful it must be. I long so much for that peace.

In the US, people have therapy as much as we go to Tesco. There is no shame in it. Maybe now it's time I strip it all back, not only be strong on the outside but on the inside too. Nothing changes if nothing changes.

'It's not you, it's me,' those dreaded words we all are so scared of hearing. Usually, they are said to us as an excuse, the old cliché to end a relationship when they can't think of a good enough reason or just don't have the capability to be honest.

I'm stubborn, I overthink and often jump to conclusions. A lot of the time, these conclusions aren't correct, but I also long to be right. Thankfully I've learnt over the years to admit when I'm wrong and apologise.

It would be so much simpler if all men were arseholes, and many I have come across are! But – and yes, there is a but – not all of them are. I've been hurt more than I care to remember, been promised the world only for it to be quite literally smashed to pieces in front of me. So now I see every man I come across as a threat, someone who is no doubt going to hurt me. The pain you get from heartbreak is suffocating, debilitating, something I don't care to feel again. But is this guarded fortress any less painful in the long run?

I've walked around for years now pretending I'm OK, that I'm OK alone, and I am. That doesn't mean that's what I genuinely want. But recently, I've realised that the wall I put up for others, I'm actually facing myself. When asked to describe my wall to a friend, I said how bad I felt for the guy I was talking to. She asked me, 'Is it not bad for you?' I didn't really understand what she meant at the time. I saw the wall protecting me, when in fact, it's been stopping me.

Growing up is both amazing and frightening. You come to understand yourself in a way you never have before, yet you have to deal with all scars that you didn't even know existed. I now realise that if you don't address them, they only get infected and cause the same debilitating pain that you're so badly trying to avoid.

It's no longer a sink or swim situation, only a swim. When I first got clean, I was told you needed to get clean for yourself or it wouldn't work. I didn't get clean for myself; I did it for my family, and sticking with it, I started to do it for myself. This, however, is a whole different kettle of fish, as the only person I'm really harming is myself. I'm holding myself back from the love and life I long for.

I am, in fact, the wall that stands in front of me, the wall I might need to break to reach a breakthrough.

The imaginary men

'Once I had a love and it was divine,
soon found out I was losing my mind.'

Blondie

I sit here once again alone in my flat, with only the company of my long-suffering dog. I've spent my day trying my best to eat my feelings, but to no avail. I feel like the McDonalds drive-through must see me and my friend coming, recognise the car and wonder what drama has happened that day for us to grace them with our arrival.

I forced two large portions of chips and two McFlurrys on myself, not feeling hungry and only feeling more full and sick with every mouthful. If they call it eating your feelings, why the fuck doesn't it work!? I declared this to my friend with a huff and placed my head in my hands for the hundredth time in days. I felt like having a tantrum, going full Kevin and Perry on my life, screaming how utterly unfair it is. After all, they did not allocate enough ketchup to go with my chips; this seems like a serious problem if ever there was one.

Yesterday I had my first therapy session, of this round at least! I managed to squeeze at least four men into an hour's session, with no doubt more to come. I hate it when someone voices something you deep down know to be true. I'm now of an age that I'm surrounded by friends, old friends, people I went to school with, etc., etc., showcasing their happy married lives all over social media. Their first house they've bought as a couple, the numerous dates they go on, their first pet, their first pregnancy, their engagement. The list goes on. I appear to now be at an age where the adverts that appear on my social media are for apps to help you get pregnant, for breast pumps, and of course the endless anti-ageing, anti-wrinkle lotions, potions, or injections. Is it any wonder I feel left out?

I could, of course, unfollow or unfriend all of the people stated above; this, however, would leave me with very little to look at. My therapist asked me if maybe these men I seem to fall for might just be a way of getting what I actually want. She hit the nail on the head. After all, they have a penis that, as far as I'm aware, is in working order and could help produce that baby that my biological clock is telling me I must get right away. The rest, well, it is completely possible that I may have just lost my mind, in the words of Blondie, and filled in the blanks in the shapes and colours I want.

I think I sort of know this, which makes it worse. Do I really even know these men at all, or have I made up a narrative for each of them which I think fits them best? I have such a vivid imagination that I often get carried away. For years I had imagined who Soulmate was, what he was like, how in love we'd be, only to find out that he thought the same thoughts. Could it just be the case that it didn't work out because we didn't match the imaginations we had of each other? Were those belly achingly painful feelings down to us just having disappointed our own dreams? After all, if he was who I thought, it wouldn't have ended. The thought that might have been the case makes me feel quite unwell.

My two favourite films have been *Romeo and Juliet*, the one with Leonardo DiCaprio and Claire Danes, and *10 Things I Hate About You*. I didn't know until recently that the latter was also based on Shakespeare. These two films have fuelled what I see love as. The one you're not meant to be with but are so in love with, and ultimately kills himself to be with you. I mean, did no one turn round to Shakespeare and say, 'Bro, that's a bit fucked up!' The second film, again, rogue male and female battle against their feelings, ignore the bad behaviour and ultimately end up together. Why are there no films of real, healthy love? Why do we strive for the hurt and pain we see and ultimately go chasing in real life?

I look back at my boyfriend I was with before entering rehab. He was film love. We would spend all our time together in a dirty squat, and to me, this was romantic – I know, crazy! We had tattooed each other with reminders of each other, picked out baby names. Our little boy was to be called Peter, after *Peter Pan*, and the girl Aurora after *Sleeping Beauty*. He drew me countless pictures that I still have, celebrating small milestones in our relationship or simply just to tell me he loved me. Sounds romantic, eh? It wasn't real.

On the flip side of that, we would go and get checked for diseases that you got from sharing drug equipment. We would walk in the pouring rain for miles to get drugs, and we would lie and manipulate anyone around us to get more drugs. And funnily enough, when I got clean, he wasn't all that supportive. When I finally ended the relationship with my new rational brain that chose living over him, the story I made up in my head was over.

He wasn't my Leonardo DiCaprio or my Heath Ledger. He was a heroin addict who would ultimately kill me. Not so romantic! My point being I still look for this love. I may not have drugs to blame for my lucid imagination anymore, but still, it goes on.

I no longer chase the dragon for that drug hit anymore; instead, I chase it for that love. Still, now, I can't seem to realise that it's killing me.

To all the men I've imagined before – you've been truly spectacular... if only you were real.

The Croc age

Every Christmas and birthday, my dad asks what to get me. Something 'practical' is always what he says. Over the years, I've always cringed when he has said this – practical is not cool. If I needed a new coat growing up, it had to be both waterproof and warm. Sometimes the warmth was another layer attached by a zip that you could unzip when you just needed it to be waterproof. Nothing cool ever got past my dad as he continued to insist on durability and long-lasting qualities.

I've never been one to choose glamour over comfort per se, although occasionally I do battle with wearing heels, only to be wishing I'd put flip-flops in my bag by the end of the night. This Christmas, my dad was thrilled when I asked for walking boots – finally, something he could get on board with – and frankly, they've been the most useful present I got this year after being forced into yet another lockdown.

As I plucked away yet another rogue hair from my chin this morning, it dawned on me that I, too, was coming into the Croc Age. I used to work in a clothes shop that sold Crocs, and I used to look at them with dismay – why on earth would someone buy them? Then my friend who was pregnant with her second child came out sporting a pair only to say they were comfy, especially when pregnant, and she would never usually wear them out. Then another friend had some, of course only for house wear, and I borrowed them to go home in after I'd got my walking boots filthy when stuck in the mud. It dawned on me that this hideous footwear was oh so bloody comfy and, dare I say it, fucking practical!

What comes with the Croc Age is a new sense of the beginning of contentment for my body, even the chin hair. This means I'm getting older, and if I'm honest, it's a miracle I'm still alive. So, I will accept my chin hair, my age lines and my newfound love of Crocs because this means I've made it through all those bad days and survived. Often when I look in the mirror, there are so many things I grimace at, such as the new shelf above my bum or 'second bum', as I like to call it. This is apparently just love handles, something I didn't have in my twenties. The new dimples that have appeared on my bottom, that the beauty industry have told us is called cellulite. I've been told this is a completely made-up word that the beauty industry invented so they could sell us products to get rid of said cellulite.

In the 90s, your eyebrows couldn't get thin enough; these days, we're told the bushier, the better. The new fashion works in ways to sell new products to reverse what they said was acceptable only moments before. To keep up with this nonsense, we'd have to take out another mortgage. I'm currently waiting for thinner lips to come back in so I can pout with pride! Size 0 was an awful trend that many like myself longed for, only for big bums to now be the craze. It is impossible to follow all these beauty ideals without a plastic surgeon on hand and a pot full of gold. And you're probably just as likely to find a pot of gold and leprechaun at the end of a rainbow.

Of course, I'm not saying that I'm about to parade around with hair where I don't want it or go completely au natural. But I am at a place where if I want a pair of Crocs, I'm going to fucking buy them, and if I buy things that are more practical than cool, I'm OK with that.

I will still no doubt compare myself to others and wish I was cooler than I am. But I'm happy that I'm on my way to some sort of peace within myself, and if the journey to that is chin hair, wrinkles and a second bum, I'm OK with that.

Right now, I'm in the most beautiful spot called Dancing Ledge in Swanage, Dorset. I have a view of the ocean and my dog on my lap, watching as my friend tries to catch some fish. I do not look cool; I have multiple layers of thermals, no makeup on, with the sun shining down on me. The Croc Age isn't all bad: you begin to see beauty all around you, on the inside of people and on the inside of yourself. This is all I've ever longed for, and it seems, finally, that journey has begun.

Comparison is the thief of joy... and comfy footwear.

Valentine's

Valentine's, Palentine's, or how I'm naming it... Independence Day! I'm not going to lie, the constant flurry of adverts, and soon-to-be loved-up social media posts, do affect me. I'm also aware that they've affected me when I've been in the wrong relationships and that a lot of the PDAs are bollocks. However, this doesn't mean that it doesn't leave you with a sinking feeling in your stomach when you see them. No one puts their arguments up for people to see that they had to force their other half to buy those flowers or all the annoying things they do.

I've been in relationships with people that thought Valentine's was bullshit; it a hundred per cent is, but that doesn't mean it's not nice to show some sort of appreciation for one another on that day. We should show appreciation every day to our partners, not just once or twice a year. Social media makes us have a constant fear of FOMO, feeds our self-doubt and all our insecurities, but we still fucking scroll through it!

This year I am single. I don't even know the next dick I'm getting as I've tried to promise myself that I'll start moving forward instead of trying to reignite past flames. They're in the past for a reason, and unless they somehow seriously sort their shit out, that's where they're going to stay... fresh dick only, please!

I feel extremely grateful to be able to spend Valentine's with some girlfriends who either don't have partners or are choosing not to spend it with them. And while this will be lovely, I know I'll still experience some sadness at the fact I've not managed to find someone who I can share that day with.

I think I've been going back to old flames for so long because I already know them. I know some aren't good for me, but I know I won't get surprised when they let me down. The fear of having to meet someone completely brand new is terrifying, knowing I could get my heart broken all over again. It's that uncomfortable comfort zone that I nestle into, too scared of fresh pain and heartache.

So, this year I have to choose myself. Choose myself over toxic men, choose myself over people that don't know how to treat me. Know my worth for the first time in my life and know that no man will make this any better. This comes from within and the sooner I realise this, the better!

So, this Valentine's, I promise to be kind to myself, be gentle with myself and have faith that everything will turn out exactly how it's meant to. And this year, I'm beyond grateful that I have women in my life who I have the privilege to spend this bullshit day of love with.

Parenting

No, I haven't suddenly become impregnated, quite the opposite: I've finally realised I need to parent myself. When we are young, there's a hope that we have parents, parents that love us and try to guide us on this journey they call life. They do their best, of course, but what happens when we are no longer under their wings, when our new safe place is merely ourselves?

Growing up, my parents did the best they could with what they were given. Of course, at times, it was not perfect, but whose life is? We were told certain foods weren't good for us, certain films and tv programmes weren't. I remember like it was yesterday, secretly watching Home and Away with my sisters, only to quickly change the channel when our mum or dad came in. Would they have even been able to imagine the sort of programmes on tv now? Frankly, Home and Away seems like a warm cup of cocoa in comparison.

When I left home, I remember vividly wanting all the things I wasn't allowed growing up. The food that seemed far too expensive when trying to feed a family of eight, staying up until the morning doing things I hope my parents never find out about. It's dawned on me now more than ever that they were right all along.

I was told to go outside and play and not sit in front of the tv. To not waste money on labelled food brands, and not watch tv that didn't fulfil my life.

Like many millennials, I have been obsessed with reality/

not-so-reality tv. I recently found myself hooked on Married at First Sight: Australia. It's a show where people are matched together by relationship experts and quite literally get married when they first meet each other. They follow their ongoing journey, the highs and lows and everything in between. As with most reality tv shows, they're all above average physically, and let's face it, we watch for the drama, not the happy endings. And boy, there is a lot of drama.

Living on my own, with no one here to ask, I had to ask myself, 'Is this nourishing your mind and soul?' The answer is quite simply 'no'. Not only is it giving me unrealistic expectations for how I should look, as many seemed to have had a few nips and tucks, but it also doesn't leave me feeling uplifted. I stay up until the early hours watching this, only to feel exhausted the next day. So, I decided a week before it finished that I wasn't going to buy into it anymore and just stopped. I had to parent myself, I had to look out for the little girl within me, who, more often than not, needs some fucking guidance.

I no longer look for pretty people, I look for beautiful scenery. A friend and I drove down to the coast and experienced the most beautiful sunset. We set up camp for the night, excited to see the dark night sky full of stars and a sunrise to wake up to. These are the moments that fulfil my mind, body, and spirit. The peace you get from being a few days away from a shower and walking with all your belongings on your back is the most content I ever feel. I put my body through the ultimate challenges to prove to myself how resilient I am. More often than not, I end up knee-deep in shit, having tried to take a quicker route. It's become a running joke that I manage to get stuck in something whenever we go out walking. Maybe this is my life reminding me that shortcuts don't always work and not to get stuck in life.

I've lived a life where I want to take the shortcut – in relationships, friendships, even in my bloody houseplants. I want them to have blossomed before I put any work in. I want things to land in my lap without having to work for them. I'm no shortcut, I haven't yet blossomed. I need love and nurturing, I need parenting. The rebellious child in me still longs to stay up way past my bedtime, to spend too much on rubbish things I do not need, and don't even get me started on my choice in men.

Parenting isn't easy. I have to wake up every morning and decide to look after the child in me. I have to fight everything I've ever taught myself, how I'm not worthy of love, and I don't deserve to have my dreams come true. It's a painful realisation when you realise the person standing in the way of your hopes and dreams is, in fact, you. The person who's responsible for going into the wrong relationships is you, and the only person who can change that is you. I know, it's fucked up.

'The mind is everything. What you think, you become.'

Buddha

Buddha had it right. If you think you're a piece of shit, you will become a piece of shit that attracts more pieces of shit until, eventually, you become a mound of shit. The only shit I want to find is in nature, not in my head and certainly not in the people around me. Today I choose to look after the little girl in me and try every day to convince her she is everything and she deserves everything. It might not be a shortcut to happiness, but I don't want to look back at my life and realise I could have changed it.

I will continue to look for the beauty within and not base my worth on the number on the scales.

That's not OK

Most of my life, I've very much sat on the fence with most things. I was indifferent to anything that requires an opinion that could lead to a heated discussion. In the same breath, if anyone was to speak badly of my friends' or family's beliefs, I would defend them to the core. My beliefs, wants or needs? Pah... did they really matter?

YES... fucking finally! Something has sparked inside of me, a rocket has been shoved up my arsehole, which is pink, by the way – apparently, not everyone's is. Something deep inside of me has said, 'I matter, I don't deserve to be spoken to badly or treated badly.'

I will do almost anything for an easy life, argument-free and hassle-free. It has come to my attention that this has only led me to be inauthentic. I've not been saying my truth because, frankly, I've never thought it mattered. Recently I finally said those three words, 'That's not OK', and what's more, I believed them. I believed that I didn't deserve to be spoken to in that way, that I didn't deserve to be treated in that way, because I am worth more.

This is worlds away from the girl who stood naked in Weekend Offender's bathroom, listening to him on the phone to his girlfriend. That girl went back to him for more mediocre sex because that's all she thought she deserved. So far away from pleading with someone who had stolen my car on a drugs binge to stay with me because that's all I thought I deserved.

My taste in men has represented what I think I deserve. Today I know I deserve better. This is a journey, and a bumpy one at that. Tomorrow I may find a new wrong'un to obsess over and take a few steps back in this journey. Today I've moved mountains. We deserve so much more than we think.

This is 31

I really wish I was here to say I'd had some sort of epiphany, a spiritual awakening, and had stopped all my old ways. Maybe I'm expecting a little too much from myself.

It's baby fever out there, it's wedding fever, it's surely-you-must-be-dating fever. It's taking me a while to adjust to my newfound celibacy and ultimate single status. It's taking everyone else around me a hell of a lot longer. Not only am I trying to convince myself on a daily basis I'm an independent warrior queen, but I'm also now having to explain to people around me why this is OK.

Were we all dropped on our heads at birth? Have we really all been conditioned to thinking that if we're not in a couple, we must be crying in the corner, longing for that other half to complete us?! It's fucking infuriating. In a matter of weeks, I've been asked if I'd like to get married and where I'd like to get married by separate people. The only response I've come up with is, 'I think I might see if there's someone I might like to marry first.' Have our lives become so boring that we can't think of anything else to talk about?

After my birthday lunch with my girlfriends, I had an emotional breakdown. It was overdue, as I didn't externally have one on my 30th. I had a breakdown last year also but didn't weep on my friends as I said goodbye, mainly because I wasn't able to see them.

Did I think things would have changed this year? That I would somehow be where all my friends appeared to be?

Maybe, but I feel I'm somewhere better. I may not have what they have, but I'm slowly but surely having the best relationship I've had, with myself. I know, cringe, but fuck it, it's true.

It's been roughly 10 months since I've been in a proper relationship. Yes, there have been slip-ups, but I can happily say I've been single for 10 months. Now nearly half that time, I've been celibate, which I think I really deserve some sort of 'celibacy shower' for. Do you think that could catch on?

For my birthday I got the one present that represented this new phase in my life I'm going into. I got a pair of Crocs! They're hideous yet comfortable footwear and will no doubt act as a chastity belt. But this is 31.

31 is...

- Dying your hair pink again, because you can't be old and have pink hair
- Trying to embrace your second bum
- Realising you're not a teenager
- Finding out from your friend's 17-year-old you are, in fact, basic!
- Realising my boobs were bigger when I was a baby
- Being a proud dog mum to my boy
- Still occasionally speaking to fuckboys
- Regretting speaking to said fuckboys
- Appreciating my beautiful friends and family for listening to me go on about all the things stated above
- Feeling grateful to be alive

Nowhere Fast

I feel as if I'm in some sort of purgatory, neither in heaven nor hell, some days just purely existing, a hamster on a wheel going round and round, wondering if I'm trying to get somewhere or find a way of getting off.

In my fridge, I currently have:

- Avocado, which I don't even like but am told they're good for me

- On the Beach mocktail – not even my drinks have sex in them anymore, or cock, for that matter

- Cheese

- Coconut milk

- Ketchup

Now I'm no psychiatrist, but I think it's a fair bet to say the person who this fridge belongs to has not got her shit together. I'd also safely say she's having some pretty shocking meals.

I manage to even kid myself: when preparing my microwave meal for one, I always put it in one of my nice bowls. It's like I'm trying to convince myself I made it or that I have some small amount of my life in order. I drink Neals Yard 'Quiet Time' tea, and I have a cleaner once a fortnight. On the outside, I'm fucking winning at this thing called life.

What's not on my highlight reel is the parking ticket I got

for parking outside my own home – I'd forgotten to renew my permit. The 100+ selfies I have on my phone that didn't quite make it to my Instagram story. The fact I still check Soulmate's social media to try and get some sort of understanding of where he's at. That I check if The Young One looks at my stories, only to be disappointed when he hasn't. The fact I put up a fucking story at all, I mean, what even is that shit? I know I'm really up shit creek when Weekend Offender gets in contact, and I agree to go on a date with him... call the fucking asylum, I have lost the plot.

I want it to look like I'm OK; I don't want people to see that I'm vulnerable. I don't want people to know I don't brush off their incessant comments about my current relationship status. That when the hundredth person says, 'Don't worry, you'll meet someone' after you just told them you're happy alone, it makes you want to scream into a pillow and then hit them with it.

I feel like I spend my days not only convincing myself that I am perfect on my own but also everyone around me. I've come to like my own space, the way I put my scatter cushions on the other side of the bed, which keeps the duvet from going everywhere and ultimately cuts down time on making my bed. I like that I don't need to hold in farts, that I can wear the most hideous underwear, knowing I'm safe from critical eyes. My sofa is for me and my boy, and we don't need to share or make space for anyone else.

So, I'm in this weird middle ground going nowhere fast, wondering how everyone gets through life putting their clothes on the right way round. Apparently, it's not something I'm always skilled at.

I want to be bossing this single she-wolf thing, I want to prove to myself I can do it. Right now, I'm dating myself, but not quite ready to commit and give up all the old fuckboys. I'm sitting on the edge of the dicksand, wondering if I should get out or jump in.

I flashback to a memory. It's 2005, and I'm 15 years old. I'm wearing short shorts and a bikini top, with 'I love Incubus' written on my chest. I'm at Reading Festival on a cocktail of drugs, thinking I've got my shit together. I, of course, didn't have anything together, and it didn't take me long to lose my shoes and have to go to one of the charity tents to get free clothes because it had begun to rain.

The song I heard them play then still rings true.

Will I ever get to where I'm going?
Will I ever follow through with what I had planned?
I guess it's possible that I have been a bit distracted
And the directions for me are a lot less in demand
Will I ever get to where I'm going?
If I do, will I know when I'm there?
If the wind blew me in the right direction
Would I even care?
I would
I take a look around
It's evident the scene has changed
And there are times when I feel improved upon the past
Then there are times when I can't seem to understand at all
And yes, it seems as though I'm going nowhere
Really fucking fast.

Incubus

Square peg - round hole

For as long as I can remember, I've tried to be somebody else. The earliest memory of trying to be someone else was, of course, my want to be a nun when I was little. I was convinced my parents would love me more and would ultimately give me all the love and attention. Surprisingly this didn't work.

Growing up, I craved to be someone else, prettier, skinnier, funnier, the list was endless. I remember wanting speech therapy for most of my teens and into my twenties because it wasn't 'cool' to speak well. I wanted to be 'normal' to blend in, to not sound like the snob the kids at school presumed I was. I managed to adopt my own muddled accent over the years. Somewhere between posh and Reading gangster depending on what I was saying. Since moving to Wiltshire, it appears I've added a West Country twang to the mix.

I'm pleased to say I've not been to many weddings over the years. My circle's small, and I have no plans to expand it. For years I've battled every time someone gets married; my need to look a certain way, the way people look at weddings, causes me to have many a breakdown. When my sister got married, I ordered so many dresses my postman became a regular and looked at me in disbelief when I tried to explain I was looking for a dress. Men seem to have it so easy – rock up in a nice suit, done.

I still look at myself in photos of that day and can see how uncomfortable I felt. Wearing a dress and heels just never feels quite right. It's not me. I managed to mould myself slightly over the years, feeling slightly better but knowing I may as well put a clown outfit on. I'm not showing who I am, only how I think I'm meant to be seen.

It's two sleeps until one more of my beautiful friends gets married. So far, I think I've spent £700 on various dresses and shoes trying to put myself in a round hole. I've wanted so much to look the part for her, to look smart. I've forgotten that if I'm not comfortable, I won't be smiling, I won't be laughing, I'll be so self-obsessed I'll look like there's a broom shoved up my arse.

I've tried to jam my growing lockdown bottom into more bits of fabric than I've had dates. I've got stuck in dresses and had to get my friends to help me out of them. I've tried so hard to be someone I'm not that I've forgotten to embrace what I am.

I may not be the dainty little woman who looks the part with the fascinator and can curtsy and speak eloquently – I'm so much more than that.

I'm a fiercely loyal and loving friend who genuinely feels overjoyed to be part of such a special day. I'm present and would slash many a tyre for the ones I hold dear. I'm there with you in your highs, your lows, and your laughter. I will take the toilet paper off your shoe when no one is looking and save you from that annoying relative. I am more than a decoration.

I wish I had embraced my differences. Now I can, now we all can. Once we accept ourselves, we begin to be who we really are, who we've been all along.

I am a square peg, I do not wish to fit into any round holes.

Pause

I'm pressing pause. On my thoughts, on expectations, on dating, on life. Unfortunately, I cannot press pause on ageing, or I'd be sure to do that too. Too often in life, we are constantly wanting, without ever appreciating what's right in front of us.

I was able to go to my friend's wedding without being in complete self-obsession about my outfit and was able to be present for such a momentous day. Not only were my friends getting married, but it was the first time any of us had been able to socialise with so many people. The number of guests at a wedding had only just been raised to thirty, and many of us appeared to be like caged animals dying to get out.

As is customary at all weddings, it appears, the singles are established early on to see who they can be matched with. Both men that are single are alcoholics, one doesn't appear to realise, and one tells me every time he's drunk enough. He confessed he was giving up as of tomorrow; this appears to be my kryptonite.

I spent most of the evening obsessing over said man, thinking maybe he could be the one. As the night went on, I watched him take a small bag of white powder to the toilet, and something clicked. For the first time in, well, ever, I thought, 'No, not for me, I deserve better.' Old me, and yes, even sober me would have mounted him. Bitten his ear, even begged him to sleep with me. My self-worth really has been that low. Tonight was different: I had a moment of clarity, I paused.

I felt empowered that evening. I wasn't going to wake up tomorrow with regrets. Every married person I spoke to told me how they hadn't had sex in months, one even admitting that she doesn't find her husband attractive and only does it when she's wasted. I was so grateful not to be married.

The following day I seemed to be on some sort of comedown. Suddenly the old me started rearing her ugly head. I felt alone. Sundays appear to be the longest day of the week when living alone. Your friends are mostly busy with family, and you're left eating ice cream straight from the tub, tempted to cry along with Bridget Jones.

I endlessly scroll through Instagram, looking at the so-called perfect lives of the people around me. Yet another baby scan picture decorates my feed. Social media may as well be adverts – they make you think you want and need what is pictured and are incomplete without it.

It's time to really hit PAUSE! My therapist questioned whether I had ever taken a social media break, having just told her of my latest upset when stalking someone I still wasn't in a relationship with. She was right; it was making me so unhappy and a little bit loco, to be honest. I really didn't want to know where my ex's girlfriend's sister and brother-in-law went on holiday in 2002.

I had stopped living and was just existing. My life is fucking amazing, and I was sitting there feeling sad about everything I didn't have rather than looking at what I did have.

The sun decided to finally shine, and I decided to brave paddle boarding with a friend. As we pumped up our boards, I saw someone I knew in the park playing with their kids. I looked at them, then back at me and my friend and smiled with my whole body. I suddenly saw everything clearly.

Only you can decide whether to be positive or negative.

- I live alone
- No one depends on me
- I sleep alone

Today these things are what liberate me. For the first time in my life, I feel free.

Reformed townie

I loved the bright lights, the hustle and bustle of the town I grew up in. I loved all the different shops and 'Smelly Alley' for its name and the shop down it that sold bongs and latex get-ups. I loved walking through the streets at night, sitting down and talking to the people begging to find out their life stories. I longed for mine to be as interesting, I longed to be interesting.

After moving to what I called the countryside, I felt I had turned my back on this life. I felt I no longer was as interesting because I no longer lived somewhere I thought to be exciting.

So, I thought it time I went back, dip my toe into the colourful pool that Reading appeared to be in my head. I had started chatting to the second person I had slept with, from said town. He had liked one of my pictures on Instagram, and as per usual, I pondered about making the first move. I had recently downloaded a 'motivation app' which came up with encouraging phrases every time I went to my home screen. It said, 'Don't overthink, just do,' so I did, I sent the message.

After going back and forth a bit, we arranged to meet. I hadn't been into Reading town centre for what was probably a decade. My anxiety always ran away with me, and I thought I would bump into people I had pissed off or would somehow slip into some heroin squat vortex, unable to get out. Strangely neither happened.

He was running late, so I pulled up my big girl pants and took myself on a trip down memory lane. To my surprise, it didn't look all that different, and no one jumped out to shout at me for mistakes I made 13 years ago. No one cared, no one recognised me, and I didn't recognise anyone either. That was the thing: you could be anonymous there, it was the drugs that made me think I wasn't.

Smelly Alley was no longer smelly, the fishmonger had shut down. 'Rock a Round', where my sister and I bought our vintage clothes and flared cords that we always had taken up, had long since been boarded up. The London Camera Exchange, where I sold my much-loved camera for drugs, was there but had since modernised their collection.

And then there was the boy, who once seemed so mysterious. He was now a man with the start of a receding hairline. Don't get me wrong, it was nice seeing him, it was probably the most I ever spoke to him. This including when I thought we had dated, which thinking about it, I'm not sure he was in on.

I once longed for the interesting stories of wild nights, the parties that resembled *Scarface*, and that he had plenty of. If I'm completely honest, part of me nearly jumped into that vortex with him, where I could go to a party full of drugs and be OK. When he suggested we skip food, I suddenly woke up.

I realised I find this shit boring. I don't want to go to parties in mansions with people thinking they're Al Pacino. Their name's Tom and they went to private school. I don't get my kicks from people that can't be authentic. I don't get excited by people that need money and drugs to validate themselves.

I no longer look at the people begging on the street as interesting, I see them as sad and desperate, how I became all those years previously. With my sudden realisation, I was back on the first train, to have dinner with my mum and stepdad. To cuddle my dog and look into the field of cows they can see from their kitchen window.

What I find interesting is nature, the sky, my dog, things that leave a warm fuzzy feeling inside, not one of darkness and despair. I often would look at these people I hung around with, who all had babies, pregnancies, proposals, and husbands and wondered how the fuck they had got it so right. It's been revealed to me that I've been looking at it through rose-tinted glasses. They are living the same lives as I left them living, but they've just decorated them with society's expectations of us.

Today I love the small city I now live in. I love that I don't use drugs to mask my feelings. I love walking, and I own walking boots. I would rather be found up a mountain than in a pub.

I no longer want to be a car crash; I want to be a practical Croc. It might not slow you down when driving past, but it's a lot more comfortable.

Know your worth

Ok, I went back again, just to make doubly sure.

Know your worth, add tax, and while you're at it, add a fucking generous tip! Too many times, I've doubted my worth, thought I was lucky for a man to take a second glance at me. It's taken a long time, a lot of soul search-ing, therapy, and countless conversations with my long-suffering girlfriends, to finally start seeing my worth.

Recently a past flame came back into my life. In all hon-esty, he never completely left. I usually would hear from him every couple of months, checking in to see if I'd let him back into my life. Yes, it was still that of Weekend Of-fender. Don't judge me!

So here I was in a pretty dark place, if I'm completely hon-est, uncovering many life questions that I didn't even know existed. He just so happened to message me when I was feeling a bit vulnerable, a bit lonely and in all honesty, he was just what I needed. A distraction from the internal pain I was experiencing.

I kept him at arm's length but let him take me out on a date, the second one in four years. He seemed different, more available, more caring. It was a while before I gave in and slept with him again. It did seem different this time, more intimate, more enjoyable. He was trying hard to prove he was trustworthy.

One of my good friends told me to scratch the itch but, ultimately, put some aloe vera on it. The thing is, it wouldn't be just me he had to prove himself to, it was my tribe, my girlfriends, my family.

I noticed how my name was saved under 'M' when he sent me a screenshot of our messages, reminding me I'd said something. Some of his ex's pictures still hung in his house. If you want someone to trust you, I suggest removing the reminders of the person who was always the third party in this relationship.

But again, I ignored these, desperate to feel some love and safety, how ironic, given he usually made me feel the opposite. Why do we search for love in places we only find doubt and loneliness? I kept holding onto the fact he was trying. He seemed to message me at all times of the day, so it was doubtful a girlfriend was around, and he wanted to see me at every opportunity. He told me he missed me and said he was gutted when he wasn't able to see me one weekend when I was away.

I realised I'd be back sooner than I thought, so I messaged saying I would be able to see him on Sunday and would let him know when; he said, 'Brilliant.' I rang him on my way back and got no answer; this was enough for me to turn to my old ways. Searching social media to try and find some glimmer of dishonesty. Going on my different social media accounts to see if he had hidden his story from me. Looking up his 'ex'-girlfriend to see if I could find anything. Ultimately getting myself in a state.

He called back a few hours later and told me he'd been asleep. We chatted for a while, and then he said, 'Can I ask you something cheeky, you can say no,' which generally means, 'If you say no, I'll be pissed off.' He then went on to ask if he could stay at my house the following Saturday, while I wasn't there, after he'd been out on the piss with the lads.

In this whole time, we've only gone to sleep together once. This was the first night we went out, in a hotel. In this whole time, he's never stayed at my house, even with me in it. I've never stayed at his or felt the need to. At this point, it's very early days and definitely not a relationship. I even told him the previous week that I'm not convinced he's not sleeping with other people. Yet he thinks he can stay in my house, have a key to it, and be trusted.

Time to wake up. I was baffled – was I overreacting? There are not many people that I would let stay in my house when I'm not there, certainly not someone who has lied to me time and time again. The sort of man I want to be with doesn't ask questions like that; if anything, I want them to show that they have their shit together and don't rely on my house to crash.

I saw him the following day, but something had shifted in me. Maybe it was because he didn't pick up the phone, maybe it was because he mentioned he was with two people, then it went to three people all of a sudden. Maybe it was the utter cheek of asking to use my house as a crash pad. Whatever it was, I'm glad it happened. I don't trust this man, I doubt I ever will. My first thought at him staying in my home was whether he'd bring a girl back here. That shouldn't be what I think of.

He messaged the following day, and he knew something was up, asking if I was OK, or maybe he had a guilty conscience. Either way, I've now not heard from him for a week. Whatever the reason, this isn't the way to convince someone you're trustworthy.

Thankfully this time round, I've got a bit more self-love. I haven't allowed any of this to hurt me, it was expected.

Maybe he's done nothing wrong and just can't be bothered to make the effort. Whatever his reasoning, I've now slathered aloe vera all over the itch.

I deserve to be with someone who hasn't lied to me, who is trustworthy and present. Maybe this needed to happen, so I could finally shut the door on the 'what ifs' in my head. The door has laser beams and multiple locks and bolts around it. This door is very much closed, and now the next one can open.

The butterfly tattoo

I'm 18. I had waited so long to reach this pinnacle age, but for what? I think I hoped life might become easier or it would end sooner rather than later. I spent my days trying to be someone I wasn't. I was living with my boyfriend and a few roommates, with Weatherspoon's only a few steps away and a row of takeaway shops; I was in teenage bliss. Most days, my boyfriend chose to play his Xbox over spending time with me, so I'd often sit with one of our housemates, drinking cider and watching Louie Theroux documentaries. It was a bit like the Jeremy Kyle effect, it made me feel like I was pretty normal.

I was meant to be either working or at college, attempting to finish my photography course. I would turn up to college high and turn up to work on a comedown. I would spend most of my time hiding in the toilet, hoping no one would notice that I'd had no sleep. Weirdly I got on with the people I worked with. They were kind and welcoming and didn't seem to see the side of me I was so trying to hide. But you can't keep this facade up forever.

I had wanted for so long to get a tattoo, and finally, I was of legal age. My boss at the time decided she would come with me; I think she may have been getting one too, but to this day, it's all a bit of a blur. We decided to start the day by visiting one of our local haunts, one I had been frequenting for some years at this point, using my elder sister's ID. It seemed so much easier when I was younger; today, IDs are scanned, and it seems a lot harder to sneak your way into places, but then this was the time you could still smoke in pubs, which seems like lifetimes ago, I guess because it is.

There's nothing like starting the day early with some beers, and some food, just to show we're not like those drinkers. I remember my boyfriend at the time hated tattoos; me getting one seemed to be a little glimmer of hope. I was finally doing something I wanted without the approval of a male. I'd chosen a butterfly, I really believed at the time I was finally coming out of my cocoon. Little did I know the cocoon was closing in around me.

The tattoo shop was small and grotty, I guess it had to be to let someone who was so obviously intoxicated get tattooed. I remember being able to see everyone in the waiting area while he attempted to permanently mark my body with a reminder of this day. It wasn't long before I started feeling nauseous and had to jump up to go and throw up the burger I'd just eaten in earshot of everyone waiting. How I managed to get through that tattoo, I'll never know, and quite frankly don't remember.

The days and months that followed were only furthering my demise. I left college with no idea of what I was to do next, and I lost my job as they didn't want to take me on full-time. I later found out they'd realised I'd been stealing, and I was just lucky they never pressed charges. I lost those friendships of people that cared for me, because my drug-taking came before anyone. My boyfriend soon had enough of me when he realised I was easily led towards other men if there was a chance of getting drugs. Before I was legally drinking a year, I was sent off to rehab to try and mend the broken girl I'd become.

This girl seems so separate from the person I am now, but

I still have the same tendencies. I am drawn to any man that will blink at me, not for drugs, but for the hope of love and security.

But this is where that ends. I've been a chameleon for most of my life, moulding myself to fit around others. This doesn't work, though; neither myself nor the people around me end up happy because none of it's real.

Yesterday I accomplished something amazing. It was a massive turning point for me. I filled my car tyres up with air and reset my car so the warning light was no longer on. Please feel free to laugh at this point, I know it sounds fucking ridiculous. I've spent my life saying, 'I don't know' and being led by other people because I haven't thought I was capable of doing it myself. I was scared to attempt to fill my tyres with air in case I did it wrong, people laughed at me, or I put water in them by mistake. It's so much easier to ask someone, to get someone else to do these things for you, but it leaves you with zero self-worth.

Today I made another decision, to stop living in the past. For some reason, I still have conversations from all my exes, fleeting romances, and dates still on my phone. I've come to realise this is also another act of self-harm. A constant reminder that they didn't choose me because I wasn't good enough. Today I deleted all those messages, one's I'd clung onto thinking maybe we'll look back at them on our wedding day and be able to show everyone how it first started. Yes, I know I'm living in a fucking dream world, and it's time to get real.

Since that day when I was 18, I've continued to decorate my body with reminders of where I've been, or who I've been with. I don't regret any of them because they remind me where I was at the time. Happy, unhappy, fucking crazy, and everything in between.

I've now been single for longer than I've been in 15 years, and whilst I still get the green-eyed monster when looking at my friends in their relationships, I know I'm exactly where I need to be. I'm in a relationship with myself, my true authentic self. Not the shell of a person I've been for all these years, desperately trying to find a man to complete me. I am complete.

Finally, the tattoo came true. I have brushed off my cocoon of men and have become my true self, that butterfly I thought I saw a glimmer of all those years ago.

Porsche the pussy

Wow, I don't even know where to begin. I've just spent the weekend with two beautiful women that I'm lucky enough to call my friends in the most idyllic setting. This journey didn't start off too smoothly; I had a dream about Soulmate, no doubt because I was about to spend the weekend only half an hour away from him. This is the closest I've been to him since we broke up over two years ago.

It's crazy how we romanticise relationships, only remember the good, and somehow forget the pain and hurt they caused us. But with these two unbelievably strong women by my side, I felt I could face whatever this weekend threw at me. This weekend didn't throw any cock my way, only pussy!

If you've got a weak stomach or easily cringe, you may want to stop reading, or maybe you shouldn't have got this far in the book. But please tell that part of yourself to do one, and come join me and celebrate all things female!

We so easily look at ourselves in the mirror and look at every small minute detail that we don't like, but how often do we look at ourselves right in the eye and say, 'I love you'? I know, extremely cringe, but extremely important. I struggle to look myself in the eyes, the same way I would look at someone I have wronged because guess what? I constantly wrong myself. I don't ever thank myself or nurture myself for the constant shit I put not only my body but my mind through. This has to stop.

This weekend I embarked on an adventure of self-discovery and a bit more acceptance. We were going to a yoga festival. Now I'm the first to admit I was expecting teeny tiny yogis that were probably so up their own arses they couldn't see the light. I'm so pleased to say I am actually a judgmental twat, because it was the complete opposite,

I saw so many beautiful bodies of all shapes and sizes. People wearing their bodies like the warriors they are. Embracing their curves, wearing whatever they wanted, and their love and confidence shining through. To say it was beautiful is a massive understatement. It was life-changing for me.

I criticise every lump, bump, mark, and wrinkle but very often forget to judge what's on the inside. Today I can say I'm a pretty good person. I'm a good friend, sister, daughter and adoptive mum to a growing brood. It's taken me many years to say something so positive about myself, but it's true.

This weekend has shown me how people's personalities shine through. It really doesn't matter what you look like, but how you act is paramount.

So, who is Porsche? She's not my new cat. She is that part of me that lies between my legs… my vagina, foo foo, fanny, minge (an oldie but a goodie!), she is whatever the fuck I care to call her because she's mine. She is beautiful, she is part of me, she is not a separate entity, or something I should ever feel shame or embarrassment for. She is a source of pleasure and sometimes of pain.

With our guards slowly dropping, we decided to go to a 'pussy gazing' workshop. It really was what it said on the tin and so much more. We lay with at least thirty other women, ready to look at our pussies in a mirror. Some of us giggled as if we were schoolgirls again, some looked a tad terrified, and some people apparently hadn't realised quite how literal the name of the class was.

We were told how often we are made to feel embarrassed of our Porsches. How we need to reconnect with them. Firstly, we were told to look ourselves deep in the eye; how I found this more difficult than looking at Porsche, I'm not quite sure, but I did. We did a fair bit of breathing before we got down to business and stared straight at our pussies.

I suddenly felt bad. How many dickheads have I let go near Porsche? How many times have I constricted her in tight, uncomfortable pants, waxed her, shaved her? I'm surprised she hasn't closed up on me as some sort of protest. But there she stays, working as she should, being this amazing organ that is the epitome of my womanhood. So, there we made a promise to our pussies and, if comfortable, to shout them out. Of course, I was the first one! I shouted at the top of my voice, 'I won't let dickheads near you.' As I'm writing this, I realise I will allow the head of dicks near her. I'm not turning to women or abstinence. My choice of words was not so great. Nice heads of dicks are welcome, horrible heads of dicks, you are banned. Only I could overcomplicate an affirmation and promise to my pussy!

This workshop was mind-blowing, and my and my friends' boundaries did not end there. After this, we decided we needed each other to check out the goods. In our tipi, we now had Porsche, Mitsi, and Rebel. Ladies, name your vagina what you want, go wild. Ours appear to go in a car theme.

So here we are, three women bottom naked in a tipi at a

yoga festival, stone-cold sober, inspecting what lies between our legs. This too was quite earth-shattering. We seemed to want approval from each other that ours were normal, not deformed or ugly. How we can even begin to describe any part of our bodies as ugly really needs to stop. We are unique. Some of us have innies, some outies, and no, I'm not talking about your belly button, have a google. Some hairy, some shaved, different shapes and sizes, but all beautiful, functioning womanly vaginas.

So, whether you call it after a car, a flower, or a cake, learn to love that part of you that we so easily shy away from. Don't just look at her when you think there's a bump or a rash. Be kind to her and embrace her as part of you, don't separate her from the rest of your beautiful bodies.

I have now seen more women naked than I have men in recent weeks. These women are beautiful; we are still growing, and we are still learning.

To put it simply, if you're worried about whether or not your pussy is attractive, look into your eyes, look into your soul. Are you kind? Are you honest? Are you trying your best? If the answer is yes, I can safely say your pussy is fucking magnificent.

Go forth and look at her, tell her…

Thank you,

I'm sorry,

Please forgive me,

I love you.

Ho'oponopono prayer

Original gent

Where are all the gents at? These days, sometimes just walking down the road can cause the most robust woman to want to have a breakdown. There's been this argument about catcalling going on for years. Many men claim women would be upset if it never happened to them, but they've never had to experience it.

I look at these men that turn their heads, stare out of their windows, and often beep. What are they expecting? Shall I run after them, declare my love and tell them I'm at their mercy? If someone actually did that, what would they do? I, for one, would want a front-row seat to see the panic set in on their faces. Shall I throw my number in a paper aeroplane, or more honestly, a note telling them to fuck off?

Men just don't get it, they think it's flattering, but when it's the tenth person in a hundred-metre walk, it gets exhausting. Can we no longer walk down the street and not feel violated? One of my sisters had so much abuse from men in this way she decided to move to the other side of the world, to a place where catcalling is actually illegal.

My grandpa will always be my original gent. Don't get me wrong, some of his views were straight out of the dark ages, but I know for sure he would never behave in this way. When did this start? When did it become acceptable for men to behave in this way?

This morning as I walk to work, again, I get turned heads and drooling faces, but having grown up a tad, I chose to ignore them these days. I remember a van of men beeping at me when I was about 14; again, looking back, this is pretty fucked up. With all my sass, I turned around and put my middle finger up at them and shouted, 'Fuck off' at the top of my voice. What I hadn't realised is one of my friends' dads had been walking by; he already didn't like me, and this, I think, confirmed his feelings even more.

But then a glimmer of hope, only in the form of an elderly gentleman. We were about to cross paths on the pavement when he encouraged me to stay on the inside, as he can see the traffic coming towards him. Have we just stopped teaching our sons how to behave? Will the gentleman-like behaviour be something we only see in history books?

Please raise your sons to love and respect women. If you don't, no one will.

Life

There was a time I longed for death, for the peace that I thought I would finally feel. Today I'm no longer there, I long for life to take me with everything it's got and show me the world.

It's midnight and I'm driving through the city decorated with people who have been out celebrating the bank holiday weekend. They're swaying, laughing, joking, and some are shouting. I'm driving home after being at the hospital. Usually, if I told anyone this, they would presume I'd been there with whatever man was in my life that had no doubt caused themselves an injury from too much alcohol or drugs. Today, my life isn't like that.

Watching life leave someone is both painful and beautiful. As my friend's mum lay there taking her last breaths, I felt elated for her; she had battled through so much. She had battled alcoholism and children dying. She had survived her worst days and could go to sleep knowing this.

What a beautiful thing is it to know you succeeded when you thought you couldn't. That you lived through the most agonising situations, and you survived. With many people now rallying round to say goodbye, I thought how wonderful it was to be so loved.

I would have done anything to share those last moments with my grandpa, to have had my family around me to hold tight. But I had this same friend by my side, giving me everything I needed. I'm so grateful I experienced this loss to prepare me for the grief she was experiencing. I've been lucky to not experience any other great losses in my adult life. When my grandpa died, it floored me. No amount of people telling me he lived to a good age was going to take away the grief and emptiness I felt. I felt like my friend put me in a cocoon and nurtured me until I was able to see the sunshine again. Without her, I don't know what I would have done.

This in itself is so wonderful, how I've gone from being in these toxic relationships, trying to fix people that didn't want to be fixed, to being able to receive and give love to someone that's present.

Whilst up at the hospital making tea, I felt a presence behind me. Not a spirit, I'm afraid, but an elderly gentleman that had decided he too wanted freedom. Unfortunately for myself and the nurses around me, it was the freedom to be naked. However scarred I now am from this experience, and possibly in need of seeing a younger penis ASAP, I couldn't help but understand.

When I'm old, I'll be like the guy in the next cubicle trying to escape, I'll be like the naked man wanting to be free. Let's face it, my friend and I will probably be streaking naked through the hospital and escaping all at the same time. We will have lived such an unrestricted life that a hospital will be like a prison. And if I'm neither of those, I will be like my dear friend's mum, taking the morphine like a trouper, finally able to feel that numbness I used to long for. When I'm ready for that, I hope and pray that I can rest safely, knowing I was able to achieve all of the things she did and survive.

Tell the people around you that you love them. Live life to the fullest. Experience everything, the good, the bad, the ugly, and the downright painful. Without the pain, you aren't living. We only get one life, so make it one you're proud of.

For our loved ones

that fill the sky

with stars.

Single woman

Independent woman, as I like to call it, but are we all really that independent? I hate to think that in this day and age, we can't act just like men and not be treated the same. Going to a car garage, having tradesmen over, or simply walking home alone can cause severe anxiety to a lot of women, more than I like to admit.

I've always been quite happy walking home alone, mainly because I'm not smashed and have my wits about me. With every day comes a new news article about a woman being violated in one way or another. Most recently, I read about how a rapist lured women into a trap by leaving a baby seat in a lay-by. Not having children or lack of any common sense, or maybe maternal instinct, I was baffled why anyone would stop for this. Apparently, as many of my friends told me, they would be worried a baby had been left. Go figure. I live in a world of my own where I can't accept or understand this sort of horrible shit that happens. Maybe it's because I don't want to.

It's become apparent to me that if you are a 'single woman', you are fair game to anyone and everyone. A friend told me how she used to borrow her friend's husband to go to car garages so she didn't get screwed over. They must see us as these delicate little flowers that they can fuck over whenever they like.

All too many times, tradesmen have spoken to whatever boyfriend I was with, forgetting I was the one to contact them and it was, in fact, my home and not theirs. Is there some sort of telepathic penis talk I don't know about?

Why, as women, do we feel we need to be chaperoned? One friend would have a selection of men's toiletries to leave out when workmen came round. Maybe we should all leave garlic round our front doors to keep the emotional vampires out. I was shocked when she told me this and disgusted, not at her but at the fact she felt this was necessary.

But does she have a point? I seem to attract gutter talk from the older gentleman; I promise you, I don't start it. I'm very careful who I'm open with about sex, as I'm already aware blinking at men can be taken as a cue to feel you up. It's not.

Maybe I pretend it doesn't happen because, in fact, I don't want it to be. My neighbour, who's similar to my parents' age, decided to talk to me about how he wished he had a sixteen-inch 'you know what', and another man spoke about someone wanting to cum in their own mouth. Hands up, looking back, I should have made it clear that I didn't find either of these conversations comfortable, but why the fuck should I?!

Is it not normal human behaviour to not talk to someone that could be your child about cum, and the size of your penis? Or have I been living in a convent my whole life? I should be able to have a fag out of my back door without having an image of my neighbour's, no doubt, tiny penis.

Who is raising these men? I don't want to put men's toiletries in my house or have an imaginary boyfriend. I'm not a bush a man ultimately pisses on to mark his territory. I've got my own territory sorted, thanks.

I remember a man gliding his hand along my leg as I tried

to fall asleep on the train. I so wished I'd punched him in the face; I didn't, I froze. Ultimately, I got up and moved away from him without so much as a cross word. No doubt he's carried on feeling women up that don't have men there pissing all over their territory, figuratively speaking, of course.

I recently took up boxing training, not to compete, but so for the first time I felt I could stand my ground. I don't want women to feel they need a man to escort them everywhere they go – it's not 1920.

We own our own houses, we work full time, we are single parents, we are powerful fucking Goddesses. I just don't understand who taught us to be so submissive.

I really hope that with practice, I'm able to stand my ground and say when something makes me feel uncomfortable. To tell people 'That is not OK.'

If you wouldn't treat your daughter like that, don't treat other women like it. We are not here to add to your wank bank.

I may start talking to them about menstrual cups and chin hair – that's sure to make them run a mile.

Friends that are family

I talk about friends that are my family, and they are, but they are always going to be more like siblings than slip into that 'significant other' slot. I thought this was enough, and a lot of the time, it is.

I love my sisters with every bit of my being, but we wouldn't stop living our lives for one another. One has moved to the other side of the world to fulfil her dreams, one has quit her job to walk the Camino de Santiago. They, of course, should do these things; we only have one life, and we must live it.

With my friends I think I was under the illusion it was different. I was trying to fill the void of a significant other with them, and it's just dawned on me, I'm always going to be left disappointed. I can't think of it like this.

I'm called 'second mum' by many of their children, but no one will congratulate me on what a good job I've done bringing them up because, well, I haven't. I won't be invited to parents' evenings or graduations. I will always be there, but I'm not their mother or father. I'm the crazy second mum they love, but that is all I'll ever be.

My friends will still make life choices without considering me, not because they don't care for me, but because that's not realistic. They have their families, they have their husbands, partners, and their children. I will always come down pretty far on the list. They love me, but I'm not their family.

I often say I couldn't live without them; I probably could but definitely wouldn't want to. I've realised they could a hundred per cent live without me because they already have that unit.

When someone decides to get married or have a baby, they won't think about me, why the fuck would they? So, whilst I thought I was surviving on my own, maybe I wasn't after all, because I'm not really alone. I'm OK being on my own, completely alone, but it wouldn't be my choice, would it be anyone's?

So, whilst I watch as my friends' lives develop, I need to remember to live my own life. Finally be free of co-dependency. I need to do things for myself, and whilst I constantly try to fit into different friends' families and invade, am I not just avoiding looking at my own unit?

My unit consists of me and my Mojo. The dog that helped heal my broken heart. Who gave me a reason to wake up, to get dressed, and to leave my flat. Before I got him, I had lost all reason for living, breathing had become painful, and I honestly couldn't see a way out.

My unit may be small and compact and often a bit smelly (definitely more him than me), but we are a unit. I will not do anything in life without first considering him. Whilst he most probably would be happy going with the next person that gives him a sausage, unfortunately, he's stuck with me. He doesn't have much choice in the situation, but I chose him. Or maybe he did choose me – they say puppies do that, after all; however, that could be just to make these crazy humans feel better.

My unit has room for a few more faces, but I need to remember to nurture what I've got. I can't highjack my friends' ready-made families. They are beautiful and perfect just as they are, and I must continue to accept that I will always be on the outside.

This is not meant to sound as depressing as I feel it does. The grass is always greener where you water it. It might be time I got myself some grass, at least!

Fat is not a feeling

When I 'feel fat', which is more often than I'd like, it is usually nothing to do with my weight. Of course, I may have eaten too much, or I may have the monthly bloat, but more often than not, it is so much more than that.

I woke up from a dream that one of my exes had seen the error of his ways and was, in fact, in love with me. I lay in my bed next to my three stuffed animals, Elefonte, Cyril, and Pedro. I definitely did not have my ex there, only my three comforting toys that, at 31, I refuse to remove from my bed, and just as well as I needed a bit of comforting.

As I do most mornings, it's time to catch up on the news, or Instagram, as many call it. I check into the work one only to find the 'nearly was' declaring his love for his girlfriend. Then a younger friend is announcing her engagement at a hotel I've always wanted to stay at but could never afford. Suddenly, I 'feel fat'.

I spend the day and the week picking myself apart. Wanting to rid myself of this feeling but refusing to give in to old ways. Instead, I question this so-called feeling and dig deeper. What's really going on with me? I hadn't felt fat the night before, so what's changed?

What's changed is I've had numerous reminders shot at me like fire arrows to the heart in fairly quick succession. I've yet again gone on the 'poor me' train and refused to get off. I've picked apart everything wrong with me and ignored everything that's right with me and, most probably, everything that's wrong with them. If my ex had come back to me and proclaimed his love, should I go back, was it right? NO. If something was a 'nearly was', maybe I just dodged a bullet. If it 'was' meant to be, it would have been. And maybe my friend is backed up with a shit load of credit card debt; after all, we only see the highlights. To be honest, the news could do with being a bit more like Instagram, and Instagram a bit more like the news. Maybe I might even start watching it.

I hate that I define myself by how tight my jeans are or whether clothes fit me. I am not a Tupperware box; I fit the same amount in me no matter my size because I evolve. I constantly get scared people will say I've gotten fatter or more wrinkly, but I don't stop and think about how they judge what's on the inside.

It's definitely an ongoing battle between the voices in my head, and maybe they will never disappear completely. My own mother still complains about her weight and she's nearing seventy. When I'm her age I want to be eating as much cake as I so wish and not care. In all honesty, this may never be me. I may also want better.

What I need to remember is to look on the inside too and want better. Better love for myself and to remind myself that regardless of how I look, if I have morals, if I have values and I continue to be my truest self, then that's all that really matters.

When you're feeling fat, maybe look a little deeper. What's really going on with you? Be kind to yourself and nurture your soul. Fat is not a feeling, no matter what we are led to believe.

The Redhead

I find myself at yet another wedding, preparing to cry myself to sleep in my hotel room, wondering why it isn't me standing in that church making those vows. After avoiding many near-death experiences on Devon's country roads, I settle in at the church with my new wingwoman I'd met whilst helping the bridesmaids get ready.

We glance around the church trying to see what available meat there is. The one I'm most attracted to is, of course, taken by what I can only describe as a woman resembling a Victoria's Secret model. The rest appear to be married off.

My dear friend getting married didn't have an easy road to get here and did have to do a bit of compromising. She hoped she would end up with a successful journalist from *The Guardian*, something I had told her might be a little too specific. Her new husband adores her, it's clear for everyone to see. I myself am beyond happy for this little cherub as she came to me almost thirteen years ago like a guardian angel.

I was eighteen and had arrived in this sleepy city to try to start a new life. I was determined to make it, but make it by myself without financial help from my doting parents. I found myself a hostel to move into, and with hardly any money to spare, I decided to go to my local food bank for some much-needed support. There she was, in charge of PR and keen to speak to me about my story.

I'm pretty sure most people would have reacted slightly differently than she did. After telling her I had been clean for maybe a month at this point, she decided to take me under her wing, invite me to dinners, gallery openings, and any social event she was going to. She even tried to get me into church. I was tempted, I'd never been to a church where you were offered coffee and cake on arrival. Not only to have but enjoy whilst you were actually in the church!

She witnessed many relationship faux pas in those early days, my need for validation had no limit. She showed me what true loving friendship was, the kind where you don't expect anything in return. Almost thirteen years later, I felt honoured to be part of her day.

She is not 'The Redhead', however. That really would spice things up! No, The Redhead was seated opposite me. With kind eyes and flowing copper hair sat a woman, a woman I couldn't keep away from.

Growing up Catholic, on the whole, I don't resent. I often have been envious of my parents' faith but not of some of the traditional Catholic beliefs. I've always tried to be open-minded, but I've struggled in recent years with everyone's need to be labelled. Has this been because I can't label myself?

I wonder if it's easier when you know you only like women, or only like men. I often hear people say bisexuals are just greedy, or confused, or haven't made their mind up yet. The word bisexual doesn't sit right with me either; I don't know if it's because I'm scared to admit it. I often say I am who I am, why is there need for a label, but is there?

I try to be open about my attraction to both men and women. I've never been a fan of watching men in porn; I don't find the male form to be very sensual. I can hear the gossip now, 'Men have fucked her over so much, she's turned to women.'

I found it so easy to talk to her, the conversation flowed. She explained how she had a girlfriend, but was in an open relationship, another thing I struggle to get my head round. Was I attracted to her because she, too, was emotionally unavailable? She explained she'd rather be in an open and honest relationship than for her partner to cheat. Does everyone cheat?

She excited me. I didn't look at her, plan our wedding and our many children. I looked at her wanting to share my body with her, I wanted her to want me. Whilst a few men paid me drunken attention, I wasn't interested.

Nothing happened between us that evening, but I know I definitely wanted it to. Did she? I don't know. How can you really tell if someone's into you? I'm still trying to work that one out.

I feel saddened that I feel embarrassed or ashamed to speak to my friends and my family about these feelings; maybe it isn't the big deal I'm making it out to be, but maybe it is.

I feel I need to explore this part of me but feel like I wouldn't know where to start. I would feel like a virgin all over again, fumbling about with, no doubt, a slightly more experienced person.

Whether I'm gay, straight, bi, or something in between, the most important thing is that I'm free. Free to be me, free to explore all my wants and desires. Free of judgment and shame.

I may never see this woman again, but she has no doubt helped me to be a little bit more comfortable with who I am. For this, I will be forever grateful to the beautiful Redhead in the suit.

Bridges

Bridges in literal and metaphorical sense have always scared me shitless. I've been known to cling onto someone for dear life, avoid, or crawl along both forms.

I was in much need of some sea air, so again, I go with my dog and walking boots in tow to clear my mind and soothe my soul. This is a fairly new hobby of mine, at least on my own. I've often doubted my ability to do almost anything alone, including walking in areas I don't already know. I decided to take myself to Lulworth Cove, somewhere I had been previously, but it wasn't to be.

I was met by standstill traffic, and while I would usually continue, something had changed; I had faith in myself. I looked at the map and decided to take a detour to Kimmeridge, knowing I may not be where I wanted to be, but where I needed to be. I parked up with the view of the ocean and salt in the air, and a much quieter surrounding. I didn't need the chaos of busy Lulworth Cove, I needed peace.

As I walk, my life's narrative constantly plays out in my head. With the wedding and The Redhead still in my mind, I try to analyse what it all means. Have I been burnt by too many men, has my promise to Porsche become all that more literal? Or have I just been presented with a new bridge?

The irony was there were so many bridges to walk over on this coastal path. I laughed to myself, wondering what my guardian angel was trying to tell me. 'Here is a bridge, one you didn't expect, but one you need to cross.' It is scary, sweat inducing, but the more I learn to accept my truth, the better I feel about myself.

When speaking to my therapist about my latest realisation, she seemed almost excited. I think, ultimately, she wants me to find my truest self, and if muff diving's where it's at, I must go forth and be true. She asked if I had contacted The Redhead; I was almost shocked that she didn't seem appalled by this idea. But how do you ask someone out? How do you tell someone you like them without being creepy?

Of course, my walk ended up being me trying to figure out what I could say, how to come off cool, calm, and collected when I was having a massive freakout inside. I eventually came up with a message that I hoped sounded all of those things.

My usual go-to would be to constantly look at whether she has read it. So far, I've chosen to eat through the panic. I've also rationalised that her response isn't the big thing here, me sending the message is. Whatever she responds, if she responds, I just hopped, skipped, and jumped over a pretty scary fucking bridge. I admitted and accepted that I find a woman attractive. I not only did that, but I told her I'd like to hang out with her.

Whatever comes from this, I looked fear in the face and told it to go fuck itself. I was true to myself and how I felt. The worst that can happen is she can say no or ignore me. If this happens, guess what? I can move on quicker without going over the endless possibilities in my mind.

When I'm walking, I feel free. Free of expectation, free of judgement, free to be fully me. Maybe this is the lesson I needed, the reminder to be fully, authentically me. It may take some time to be free with some friends and family, but I have taken the most important step: to be true to myself.

In truth lies freedom.

Control

Control – The power to influence or direct people's behaviour or the course of events.

In life, many things ultimately control us: how we were brought up, what we're surrounded with, people's belief systems, and often, relationships we get into. But what if long after those relationships have ended, we are still allowing ourselves to be controlled?

Throughout my life, certain situations and people have controlled me, mainly because I've allowed them to. Whether it has been the beliefs of my parents or my ex-boyfriends, I've allowed them all to dictate who I am. It's been nearly four years since one of those relationships ended, and I find myself still thinking of him before I act. Still allowing his wants and needs to impact my own wants and needs.

Last week an old friend messaged saying he needed me, he was broken. This was the same friend who cut all ties with me when my relationship had come to a catastrophic end. When I was in need and he was nowhere to be seen. But my old pattern showed up and told me to let him in.

I invited him round and felt on edge the whole time. I listened to his woes and gave my honest and blunt opinions. When he left I felt like I needed to smoke my flat out with sage, the bad energy was all around me. I wasn't being true to myself. I had slipped into old ways of allowing someone who has no benefit to my life to enter it once again. Maybe this is why the following day, when Weekend Offender messaged, I found it easier to stay in my truth and not answer. The pain from the previous evening was still prevalent in my mind.

I've been asked why I still keep allowing these people to control me. Am I, in fact, scared of what life may be like living in my truest form, without control or judgement?

I haven't been openly, social media open, in a relationship since the demise of my long-term relationship. I tell myself it's because I don't want to rock the boat with my ex. But it's been almost four years now; is this just a lie I'm telling myself to keep myself safe? If I were to publish my relationships and then, once again, they end badly, I feel I'm left looking like the mug.

It takes a lot to unlearn patterns that have been ingrained in you all your life. Living any form of life that's not seen as conventional will no doubt be frowned upon. Being in a new relationship will send shockwaves through the town. Is this all my ego talking once again, do people even give a shit? Would I care if it was someone else? No, because I'm too wrapped up thinking about myself.

So, whether it's my ex, my ex-friend, or a person on the train, I'm the only person that's in charge of who has control over me. Today I'm choosing to rid myself of that bad energy, wave sage all around them, and begin to live in my truest self.

Sometimes, you might be sprinting, and other times, you may have to crawl, but ultimately, you need to get to the finish line. Once you're there, you will find freedom, freedom to be whoever you so wish without the need to have approval from others.

Who am I?

'Be who you were before that stuff happened that dimmed your fucking shine.'

Author unknown

Like many, growing up was a confusing time. I was forever trying to find my tribe, my people, or just any people. At primary school, I liked chess and asking lots of questions. I was that girl who looked like she constantly needed a piss with her hand enthusiastically in the air. At play times, I was mainly alone.

In secondary school it was made abundantly clear that being eager in the classroom was not cool. Chess was not cool, neither was my Quicksilver bag, my name, and even my voice. Too posh for state school and too poor for private. Too enthusiastic, too quiet, too loud, too me. So, I muted myself, tried my best to be invisible. I got the Nike drawstring bag and gelled my hair back, leaving two strands of hair at the front. I smoked, I stopped listening in class and stopped asking questions. I dimmed my own shine to fit in with other people.

When I had boyfriends, I'd fit in with them. Wore what they wore, listened to what they listened to and thought what they thought. When I found drugs, I thought all my prayers had been answered; finally, my inner critic was silenced. Unfortunately, only until the following morning when the realisation and memory of my exploits from the previous night flashed in front of me.

Getting clean, I thought, surely this must be it, I can learn to be me. But then I continued to seek validation from men, too scared to ask myself who I really was. I allowed these men to mould me, allowed them to think they were saving me and looking after me. I allowed them to control who I was.

I'm just a little girl, looking at a woman, asking her to love me. I'm that little girl, crying from inside, begging to be loved and accepted. Finally, I think I might be hearing her.

I am not 'too' anything. I am perfectly imperfect. Today I have boundaries, because guess what? I have some self-respect. Weekend Offender messaged today, a message saying how his nan had died, he'd been in court, I wasn't that into him, so no hard feelings. Old me would have bitten, and how I wanted to. But he's not worth the response. So many times, people send messages that have a hidden message within. They want you to react, they want you to reply, even if it's for an argument. Today I say no.

It's taken me a long time to reach this level of acceptance, to know that I am enough. Know that I don't need to lower my standards to seek anyone's validation. The only validation I need is from myself.

I am not for everyone, but not everyone is for me. I like laughing, I love talking about sex, I love having sex. I love being with my friends and family but also being on my own by the ocean. I like putting makeup on, I also like looking homeless. I love healthy food and I like demolishing a whole packet of Mars Bar ice creams. I like men and I like women, I like people, I like souls. I might be crass and swear, but I happen to love the word cunt.

It's there when I need it.

I like walking for miles, and I also like lying on the sofa all day with my dog and eating my body weight in food. I like watching trashy tv, and I like watching tv that makes you think.

If anyone had told me that one day I might feel this way about myself, I would have laughed. I can look at myself in the mirror today and feel love. Love for myself, my mind, body, and spirit. Writing this, I could cry; I never thought I would ever be able to be me, the real authentic me, the one I've hidden for so long.

If I continue to look at fear and face it head-on, I will continue to fall in love with myself. By being our truest, most authentic selves, we might disappoint other people, but we can't disappoint ourselves.

I love me, I love my humour and my snort when I laugh. I love my zest for life and my love for my friends and family. I love the home I've created and the challenges I have faced.

I am closer to being me than I ever thought possible, and what a wonderful place to be.

Exposure

I've come to idyllic Devon to spend the night away with my mum. The smell of sea air always calms me right to the core. There's nothing quite like it, I feel free and full of hopes and dreams. I often envision myself in a coastal cottage with a sea view covered in a blanket and writing while I look at the wildlife go by, trying to imagine the freedom they must feel.

I definitely feel like I needed a break, having just spoken to my first potential publisher, I feel a little overwhelmed. Why would anyone want to hear what I have to say? My inner critic screams at me. The thought that my words could one day be read by people is fucking terrifying. Then the ego pays a visit: everyone I know will read it, what if my exes get angry? Somewhere in the middle is my rational self, who believes the people that need to read it will, and many, many others won't.

My mum appears to be my biggest fan. She seems to tell every passing stranger how I'm writing a book. She's not heard all of it, and I'm not entirely sure if she may change her tune on reading my innermost thoughts. Maybe if it gets published, she can sell it at her coffee mornings and church fetes; maybe these women can live through someone who has lived in the way I have and has a wardrobe full of T-shirts to prove it.

I've spent most of my life wanting to be invisible, to blend into the crowd, then there is this exposure. I lay myself bare, share my innermost thoughts, the good, the bad, and the downright ugly. How can I ever be completely OK with that, will I ever? Meeting the publisher, if I'm honest, made me want to run and hide and never to speak to her again. I'm scared, but what am I really scared of? Is it the exposure, the vulnerability I'm putting myself in? If I'm honest, no. I'm scared of failing. I'm scared of having a mediocre book that no one reads or likes. I'm scared that I'm actually not at all clever and that people will laugh at my attempt to be a writer. I can hear my English teacher's voice now, 'I told you your writing was too chatty.'

All of those people that made me feel like I was worthless have taken a front row pew in my head. They're jeering at me, raising their eyebrows, and whispering just loud enough to hear their mocking voices. Who do I think I am?

The answer: I am a nobody in a world full of somebodies, and at one point didn't even want to be a body. But I have a voice, a voice who can laugh through her mistakes and be grateful for them. I thank people for the pain they've caused me because they helped create my voice. A voice of understanding and no judgement. A voice that only hopes to comfort and not to condemn.

As I cycle from Topsham to Exmouth, peace floods my body. The smell of sun cream and freshly cut grass makes me feel like I'm in the light of summer when, in fact, November is here. With the promise of colder days and darker nights, and more reasons to snuggle up with my dog and hide away from the world. I remind myself how far I've come. I remember in my adolescence, I used to walk to the neighbouring fields and sit in the long grass to feel that same peace. When the world got too much for me to bear, that's where I found my salvation. With the faint noise of people living their own lives and birdsong, I found that inner calm. I would stay there for hours, trying to figure out what life was and why I was still here.

I found that same solace in drugs; they took me to that place but with a sure way out. So many people aren't lucky enough to get out of the big dark hole I had found myself in. I see it time and time again, people trying and failing to get clean, it's heart-breaking. So maybe it is my duty as one of the lucky ones to live my beautifully extraordinary life to the fullest. To take those risks that scare me shitless, and to maybe bring comfort to one other person that doesn't think they can make it.

I am a nobody, but I am a somebody who has a voice. I may not be social media famous, or write for a newspaper, but I write for myself. I write for those people who need a laugh, who can laugh at my misfortune and hopefully feel comforted. I write for the little girl I was, who needed this to get through. I write for that little girl because she is worth the risk.

Today I am terrified, but I have faith. Faith that no matter what, I'm right where I need to be.

Filtered

You're told to only compare yourself to the person you were yesterday, but what if you don't even recognise that person? I spent a lot of time using a beautifying filter when I was suffering with adult acne. I was so self-conscious and couldn't bear to look at photos of myself without a filter. What happened, though, is I would then compare my current skin to the skin in these photos. It took me a long time to realise my skin never actually looked like that. I was comparing my real-life face to a highly filtered face.

I often see influencers trying to normalise rolls or bad skin and showing before filters and after filters, but what if we just tried to eradicate them? Don't get me wrong, I'm not gonna start putting pictures of myself with my double chin, or take photos from a bad angle on purpose, but just try and be a bit more real.

I work in an industry where image matters, and I'm not against making the best out of what you've got, I encourage it – if you feel good about yourself, you exude confidence. I just feel that by constantly filtering and editing our photos, we're losing our grip on reality.

I remember when I did my photography course and I always preferred film cameras. I'd often find that people would take two minutes taking a basic photo then hours on photoshop making it look amazing. It used to piss me off. I don't think that's photography; to me, that's computers. I would spend hours trying to take the perfect picture and it would never measure up to the highly edited ones, much like my face.

I've decided to make a pledge to myself: I'm no longer going to filter my photographs. Sometimes this feels a bit painful. The pigmentation on my top lip, the lines round my eyes, the spots, and the scars that have been left by my compulsive picking, they scream at me to put that beautifying smoothing filter on. Yes, people may think I look good, but imagine the horror when they see me close up; they must think I've aged about ten years.

I constantly say how I want to live in my truest self; my fil-tered self isn't true. Yes, I will continue to use good angles and hope for the best lighting, but one small step may help me begin to accept myself a little bit more. It's those small steps that make the big difference. If we don't start somewhere, then we will never reach our goal.

It's much like the time I used cement-like foundation to cover my skin. Yes, I still wear makeup, but if I'm off work or not going out, I like to let my skin breathe. In lockdown, I realised that just because I didn't have makeup on didn't mean I had to finish the look with my hobo-chic attire. On many occasions I've worn a really nice outfit with a bare face. The outfit can be enough sometimes. Our true beauty shines through. And yes, it's nice to get dolled up, and I will never say never to surgery and Botox because I can't predict how I may feel in the future. I don't judge or condemn people that do these things because we've all got to do what's right for us and what makes us feel great.

It's all about us feeling beautiful in our own skin. If that's being plumped up, our greys covered and our fat drained out, and we feel great for it, amazing. If we let our body hair grow, don't wear a bra or make-up and feel beautiful, that's amazing too. But let's try not to live by filtering and editing standards that are much like chasing the dragon. We will never reach that equilibrium, it's not real.

Let's love our bodies, whatever shape, size, and amount of hair they have on them. With every scar, mark, mole, or pigmentation mark, we are all unique. Nobody else in the world has the same body as us. If we ever get kidnapped, let's make sure the photos we have of ourselves resemble us enough so they can find us.

I will continue to share my highlights, but filter-free.

Moving on

The black dog has appeared, and there seems to be no other reason for it than the nights getting darker. On Monday, my therapist told me she, too, was moving on. Our weekly sessions would become every two weeks, and she was going to live off-grid in Portugal in her newly bought camper van. I am, of course, delighted for her, but I'm left feeling like even my therapist is getting on with her life while I'm still figuring out where I fit in.

I appear to be projecting my own thoughts about my sexuality onto those around me. I've been scared to tell some of my close friends about my new realisation, and all I've been greeted with is excitement. This just leaves me to realise more that the issues I'm having are mine alone. They may have been ingrained in me from my youth, but they are definitely not the beliefs of my friends.

Today I decided to re-download a dating app, but this time my preference has been changed to everyone. To say I'm a little freaked out is an understatement. I feel like a fish out of water, not just because I haven't done this for nearly a year but also because, to be honest, I have no fucking clue what I'm doing. I may as well be a virgin all over again; it's been so long since I've spoken to new people that it's terrifying me. Added to which the whole girl-on-girl situation – how do you even do this?

I've decided to do things differently, or at least try to. I don't want to be glued to my phone, sifting through people with every spare minute I have. I do have other shit to do. They make these apps so they're addictive, and I certainly don't want to feel like it's a full-time job again. I'm in some sort of limbo, scared but feeling like I'm not living my full potential.

I have to remember that I might never meet new people if I stay in my flat watching reruns of *Friends* in my granny pants. I feel I'm at a point where I soon may grow my pubes so long that I can plait my vagina shut. I may be at a point where this uncomfortable feeling I'm having is actually good, because I need to get out of my comfort zone.

How do people even meet anymore? Do these dating apps even work? I've been on it less than a week, and it's slim pickings. I'm trying hard not to go for my usual type, even swiping right for farmer types. But guess what? I'm probably not their cup of tea. You'll be talking to someone one evening only to see they've unmatched with you by the morning. I've had little to no interest from women, yet here I am, glued to my phone once again, hoping to find the answers to life's great mysteries on fucking Bumble.

I often turn to writing when I've had some sort of epiphany about life, but truth be told, I haven't. I feel alone. Alone in a world full of people, alone in a room full of noise. I keep wondering what's wrong with me, why aren't people interested in me. I used to think it was because I didn't think I was interesting, but I actually do now. I have a lot going for me. I love my life, it is full of adventures.

Yet again, I have to trust in this process. I feel like crying into my pillow and eating until I can't move. The darkness in the sky seeps into my being, so I need to try even harder to find the light.

Today I feel alone; I hope tomorrow I'll feel whole.

One night I dreamed a dream.

As I was walking along the beach with my Lord,

across the dark sky flashed scenes from my life.

For each scene, I noticed two sets of footprints in the sand,

one belonging to me and one to my Lord.

After the last scene of my life flashed before me,

I looked back at the footprints in the sand.

I noticed that at many times along the path of my life,

especially at the very lowest and saddest times,

there was only one set of footprints.

This really troubled me, so I asked the Lord about it.

'Lord, you said once I decided to follow you,

You'd walk with me all the way.

But I noticed that during the saddest and most trouble-some times of my life,

there was only one set of footprints.

I don't understand why, when I needed You the most, You would leave me.'

He whispered, 'My precious child, I love you and will never leave you, never, ever, during your trials and testings.

When you saw only one set of footprints,

It was then that I carried you.'

Footprints

Margaret Fishback Powers

Whoever your lord may be.

Buses

I remember vividly trying to catch a bus when I was a teenager. It was pissing down with rain, and I could see it in the traffic nearing the bus stop. I ran with everything I could muster to get to it in time, but I failed. It seemed to be some sort of miracle that this bus was now stuck in traffic, so I ran on to the next bus stop, in plain sight of the driver. He saw me, I was drenched through. I got there just in time, he looked at me and drove away. Yes, I know, when did bus drivers go on power trips? This bus driver represented my dating history. Almost fucking with me, looking at me in the eye, promising warmth and security only to leave me cold and alone.

Now I'm a couple of weeks back into the dating game, and it seems the buses are back. I almost feel like a tree that one dog has pissed on, and now all the other dogs want to piss on me too. Am I sending off some sort of pheromone? I've been waiting what seems like an eternity for a bus, and now three appear at once.

Bus Number One is an all-singing, all-dancing, magnificent creature – at least, that's how I've made him appear in my head. I've not actually met him yet, only FaceTimed him, but, of course, he is the one. I'm terrified, he seems pretty perfect, and I still need to get through two more days at work to see if he is how I've imagined. He's active but not arrogant with it, not like Weekend Offender. He spends his spare time going to exhibitions and sometimes struggles to finish his second beer. I felt like proposing in that moment but thought I better try and play it cool. I mean, who the fuck can't manage two beers? I'm besotted before I've even met this poor guy. My greatest fear? He doesn't like me. More often than not, when I'm scared about this, I end up not liking them. I've got to remember if this bus doesn't stop for me, it was going the wrong way. Remind myself I'm enough, I'm amazing, I am worthy of great love. I'm writing this more to try and drum it into my head.

What I've realised is that in staying away from the dating game, I was able to avoid those deep-seated feelings of wanting that companion, that great love, the father of my children. And whilst I dive back into it, I'm reminded of that great longing that I've been trying to ignore.

Bus Number Two is funny. He seems lovely, but I'm not sure his tyres have enough air in them. It seems a bit rough round the edges, like I might need to do some oiling. However, I haven't actually met him either. All my judgement could be misplaced. He may have the savings to fix it up but doesn't have the time. Maybe he's just waiting for a reason to do it. He says he likes hiking, but I'm not sure if that's round the many pubs that grace this city. Is he, in fact, just telling me what I want to hear? Is there rust beneath the paint job? He is super keen to stop, whereas Bus Number One seems to be cruising. This bus has the doors wide open, wanting me to jump on board.

Bus Number Three, well, he's a bit of a drag racer. He's got sparkling alloys and flames painted down the side. He looks great, but he knows it. He's got a cheeky grin and isn't afraid to throw the odd insult your way. Is this bus actually negging me? So far, he's told me he thought I was older, and my dog stinks. But you still want to jump on the bus and go for a drive. You don't want to go anywhere far, maybe round the block. Scratch an itch.

Whilst one moment all buses appear to be lining up, in the next breath they vanish. Even my dog has taken to his bed to get away from me at this point. One moment I'm exuding pheromones, the next a repellent, with no sign of when it might change again.

Ultimately, I know that I'm OK, with or without the buses. I can walk. But whilst yet another person announces their pregnancy and another eternally single friend starts to settle down, I can't help but wonder when it will be my turn. Yes, I have had relationships, but as time goes on, I realise they weren't so much relationships as they were a need to be loved and cared for. I now love and care for myself, even though, at times, it feels like running up Everest. I know I deserve love.

I don't want to go into the next relationship desperate for that love because, ultimately, it will only fail. Is everyone else really that lucky, or have they settled for something mediocre? I hope they haven't settled; I don't wish that on anyone, it will plague you knowing that. To say at thirty-one that I imagined myself in this situation would be a lie. I am happy, most of the time. I have found my tribe. All that is missing is the person I hope to spend a number of years with and hopefully start a family with.

As long as I stay true to myself, and don't take any shit, hopefully the rest will fall into place. The date and time of this is still to be confirmed, much like the next bus.

No Drama

Bus Number One it is. For the past week, I feel like I've been having to have a constant word with myself. I need reminding to stay in the moment and not to self-sabotage. I survived my date; he was lovely, everything I could have ever asked for. No drama whatsoever, and it feels so alien to me. He seems secure, independent and not at all needy. 'No Drama' messages when he has something to say rather than trying to fill the constant silence. So, of course, I want to fuck it all up.

Last week I convinced myself it was a really good idea to fuck the guy who's due to do some work on my flat, Bus Number Three. I went so far as to arrange to meet him, only for my guardian angel to intervene and mess the plans up, and I was relieved. I knew I didn't actually want to sleep with him, he wasn't worthy of Porsche, but fear took over me and my old behaviour crept in. At this point, my friends feel like slamming my head into a brick wall. But I had a word with myself and reminded myself I deserve happiness.

I find myself on a second date, still no red flags, no pink flags, no flags at all. Just a perfectly nice bloke who has his shit together and seems to not think I'm too much of a dweeb after snorting with laughter on our first date. My therapist reminded me today how far I've come. The relationship I used to have with myself matched the toxicity of the relationships I had with men. Could the law of attraction really be working? Could I finally have attracted someone healthy because I have become healthy?

On my way home, I started to have a massive freakout. 'He's stripping me of my independence,' I thought, 'I'm no longer going to be that strong independent woman.' How much fucking power am I yet again giving to this poor soul? Close to changing my name and running off to Timbuktu with my friend, I decided to sleep on it. A friend reminded me that changing your name by deed poll on a Sunday was pretty hard, and you usually needed a GP to sign it off. Well, getting an appointment with one of them at the moment is nearly impossible.

I was described by a friend as pretty balanced the other day. I understand the avoidance in relationships as well as the neediness. What I realised when I woke up this morning is that I'm not so much balanced as can go from one extreme to another. Yesterday I wanted to fuck this guy off; today, I don't think he likes me. I've spent most of the day gazing at my phone, wondering why he's not obsessively messaging me; if he were, I'd no doubt be boarding that plane. It seems like I, yet again, need to have a word with myself.

I am enough. I am amazing. Ok, that's all I've got for now; this isn't always easy. I was reminded today that as long as I'm in a healthy relationship with myself, my relationships will be healthy. It appears I may need to plug more into myself at the minute, stop the crazy head from making up elaborate stories telling me he's got a wife and five kids he's not telling me about.

I've never proclaimed to like the beginnings of relationships or dating as a whole. This time I need to do things differently, I need to continue to put myself first. I need to continue to do my own thing, and if I go on a date, it's a bonus, not my reason for waking up. It's tricky – my sisters already commented on whether my name goes with his last name, and my mum, I think, was close to wetting herself when she heard I'd been on a date. My friend has already asked if I'd move to where he lives. Is it any wonder we struggle so much to live in the present?

But here I am, doing things differently. I know his full name and have not stalked him on social media. As of yet, I've not even googled him to find out if he has any criminal convictions. I'm really trying to do it the old-school way, getting to know the person in front of me instead of the persona they put out.

If anything, I've realised there are men out there that have their shit together. That these men can also be attracted to me. If this is all I learn from this flagless hero, I will have yet again gotten a blessing rather than another bloody lesson.

Stay plugged in, stay true, and stay you. Our relationships are only as healthy as the ones we have with ourselves. Today I'm choosing me.

No pain, no gain

So, I find myself seven dates in with No Drama. I've never ever made it to that number of dates before. I think I may have been on two at a push before it either ended or they swiftly moved in. I find myself in between dates losing my shit, full of anxiety, and wanting to sack it all in. But I haven't. why? I'm not entirely sure. I guess the fear of missing out on something is greater than the fear that makes me want to bolt.

I tell myself in the gym, 'No pain, no gain,' so why is this any different? Obviously, the pain shouldn't be caused by the other person involved, and in this case, it definitely isn't. It is all completely made-up stories I've told myself. It is, in fact, growing pains.

A year ago, I probably wouldn't have gone on a second date because I wasn't ready to let nice in. How weird that we become so conditioned to being treated like shit that when nice comes along, we have no fucking idea what to do with it. If nothing else comes of this, I feel so bloody lucky that I have experienced what nice feels like. I've had a man open doors for me, cook me breakfast, and bring me coffee in bed. He checks up on me, asks if he's going too fast, and even asked if his driving was OK for me. I had an ex that would drive more like a bell-end if I felt carsick. Another ex used to slap my fresh tattoos because he thought it was funny.

This doesn't feel like a rollercoaster, but a smooth ride on a gondola, being fed grapes and probably serenaded.

This feels like a warm fire on a freezing cold day. This feels so nice. 'Nice' is probably one of the most underrated words. Nice is content, nice doesn't have anxiety, nice doesn't leave you wondering what's going on.

On one of our dates, we climbed Glastonbury Tor, and he brought a picnic blanket for us to sit on. On telling my friend, she beamed, saying how she loved an organised man; it got me thinking. The most organised a man has ever been previously is by way of bringing a condom, and that was if I was fucking lucky. We both decided that I have dated a lot of dicks – I've managed to write a whole book on them.

I struggled with working out if I liked this flagless man because I wasn't feeling the adrenaline I'm so used to. That adrenaline has been my fight or flight mode, not love. It has been my whole body screaming out 'danger, fucking danger' whilst I mistook it for love. There is honestly nothing not to like about this guy; I know this sounds fucking cheesy, but it's true. I've tried to find something, anything, but so far I've come up with absolutely nothing.

Maybe this won't work out, maybe it won't be the happily ever after, but it's sure set the bar a little fucking higher. Before going to his flat for the first time, he told me how he was embarrassed by the mould in his bathroom. Firstly, I told him, you own that fucking mould, be proud. Plus, I used to live in a squat, so a little bit of mould doesn't bother me, maybe a few used needles might. Yesterday I was FaceTiming him, and I felt myself welling up. I'm planning on visiting him this weekend with my dog, and he said he'd get him his own dog bed and bowls if that would make me feel better. I mean, this guy has had the goods, if you know what I mean, and he still wants to see me.

He wants to, see, me. He doesn't just want a shag, he doesn't just want the dates. He wants to get to know me, not the surface me, but the real me. He wants adventure, and understanding, and memories. Fuck, I'm gushing, I may vomit in my mouth. But who knew these men existed? I keep asking where he came from, to which he replies, his mother's womb.

All I now know is they're out there. The ones that our lists are made of. The ones that treat us with kindness and respect. If I do end up dating anyone else, they've got a lot to live up to, because to be honest, I won't put up with anything less. I deserve this.

A week before Christmas

It's a week before Christmas, I've just spent the weekend with my boyfriend – yes, it appears I have a boyfriend for the first time in four years. We spent the weekend decorating his house and watching Christmas films; a small glimmer of hope was finally appearing for me. Could this Christmas be different?

We were going away for New Year, and it was safe to say we were in our honeymoon bliss. I haven't felt this way in so long, safe, secure, and on my way to falling in love. Whilst watching *Elf* snuggled up on the sofa, my phone started to ring. It was someone I used to be friends with. Months earlier, he had tried to reconcile with me, but he had ghosted me when my long-term boyfriend and I broke up. I couldn't be friends with someone who could leave me at my hour of need. But why was he calling? Could he just be trying again?

With no desire to ruin our early Christmas celebrations, I chose to ignore it. Unfortunately, curiosity got the better of me. He hadn't been in a good place when I spoke to him last, what if he did something stupid? I would never be able to forgive myself. So, I messaged him and asked if everything was OK. This moment in my life will haunt me until the day I die; thinking about it now gives me goosebumps. He replied telling me it was urgent, and I must call him.

The events that followed seem like a complete blur. I felt like I'd been stabbed in the heart; one minute I was cuddling up with my new boyfriend, the next I was finding out my ex-boyfriend, Prince Charming, had ended his life.

How was I meant to feel? What was I meant to do? I was finally moving on, finally in a new relationship, I thought I had broken free. I had to leave, I couldn't be here, I didn't want to be anywhere.

How I drove the hour and a half back home, I will never know. I was hysterical, I couldn't breathe. Was this some fucked-up joke? I rang him back, unable to take in what he had said. I needed him to tell me again, again and again until it sunk in. But would this ever sink in?

On the drive home, I rang my family, the people that saw him as family, that had loved him like a son and brother. I can still hear the noises that came out of my sister as if she was next to me. I was on autopilot. I just needed to get home, home to the flat that was our home, to the flat that still had so many memories in it. How could he have done this? How is it possible I will never see this man who I never truly stopped loving, the man who I spent a third of my life with, the man who I broke up with to save us both?

This must be a dream, a fucking nightmare, not my life.

THIS IS 32

New year, new pain

Somehow, I have muddled through the last couple of weeks, carried by everyone around me. Who am I in all this? Trying to navigate this grief that has taken over me whilst trying to be in a new relationship is almost impossible.

Would I want to be No Drama now? I hate to say it, but I wouldn't cope well with this situation if the shoe was on the other foot. I couldn't cope with knowing someone I'm in a relationship with was grieving someone they spent eight years with. Maybe that's my immaturity, my insecurities, but I wouldn't. So far, he's been as supportive as I guess you can be, but I've not been able to be my true self with him. I feel bad for being upset, I feel guilty for feeling lost, so in all honesty, I'm faking it all. I'm hoping that, in time, I will be able to be myself again, not this masked person I have now become.

When I'm not with him I fall apart, my zest for life has disappeared, the drugs I used to rely on starting to become a lot more appealing. Prince Charming wouldn't want this, he wouldn't want me to go down that road, but I didn't want him to do this. Why didn't he call, why didn't he scream, do something!? I'm surrounding myself with people, with my friends, my family, his family. They tell me I was the love of his life, that he never got over me, that he never loved anyone like me. However painful this is to hear, it validates my grief somehow, gives a small insight into why I'm feeling so broken. A part of my heart that belonged to him has died.

I spent my New Year's playing happy families with No Drama. I met some of his friends and tried my best to put on a reassuring front that I was OK. Should I be OK? People's judgements and opinions have started poisoning my thoughts. So many don't understand – they try but how could they?

This is not how I thought this year would be starting; the hope that this year would be different has become a distant memory. A fairytale that seems so unreachable.

The irony that I thought I'd found someone without any drama has not been lost on me. He met someone who was strong, independent, and full of life. The person I am in this moment couldn't be further from that.

Can I keep this charade up?

I am thirteen

It's now been thirteen years since I decided to start my life over. To get up when I fall, to try with everything I've got to do this fucked-up thing called life.

In the past month, my much-loved dog was nearly left paralysed, Prince Charming committed suicide, I've had a rat chew through electrical cables as well as a water pipe, and the relationship with No Drama has ended. Life happens, hard stuff ultimately tests us. Here I am, drained and, quite frankly, without any more gas in the tank.

I'm trying to work my way through a grief that doesn't make sense. One minute I'm deeply sad, the next I'm angry or just indifferent. How do you grieve someone you shared a third of your life with, who you haven't been with for four years? How do you grieve for someone who, part of the time, didn't treat you well? Why do I feel such sadness? Ultimately, how the fuck do you do this whilst in a very new relationship?

Well, looks like I don't have to worry about that last one now. The most healthy relationship I've ever been in was dealt the biggest curveball, and it doesn't appear to have survived. He blames the distance between us and my want for children, but I've not moved house since we entered into this relationship, nor has my want to have children one day changed. Does he just not like me enough, or is there something else? Maybe he doesn't even know himself.

I've come on such a long way since I embarked on therapy. The old me would be going batshit crazy, bombarding him with messages, maybe even turning up at his house, begging him to love me. But where has this ever got me? More often than not, crying to my friends over multiple tubs of Ben and Jerry's.

It's an absolute miracle that I've not used every shit situation I've found myself in as an excuse to go down the old path. Believe me, I would love nothing more than to be in the oblivion of heroin right now. Just a moment to not feel the pain that is riddled through my body. To stop the ache in my heart, to stop the feeling that, once again, I've failed. I've failed to be an adult, I've failed to make a relationship last longer than two months. Why does everyone else seem to get it so easy?

Sometimes I have to get through a minute at a time. If I went back to that, would my life be any better? No, it might just numb everything for a glorious minute. People say what doesn't kill you makes you stronger. Am I not strong enough?

My only option is to pack my bag and book a flight to my beloved Spain. Walk the next part of the Camino. I don't know if the answers are there, but aside from finding my nearest crack den, I'm out of ideas.

Again, I need to find myself amongst the pain and anguish and remind myself who I am. Dust myself off and, yet again, start again.

One day this will all make sense, I'm sure, but at this moment in time, I feel like my fairy godmother is on an acid trip. I really need to get her to rehab.

How to fail

What is it to fail? I feel yet again I have failed, failed to make a relationship last, failed to be a woman in some way. One part I hate about break-ups is having to tell people. I feel like I'm waving the 'pity me' banner, and people will look down their noses at me. I feel embarrassed that I haven't made it to the next stage, the next stage in life we're brainwashed into thinking was where we were meant to be.

I thought this relationship was it, but it was different this time. This wasn't based on lust, but on character. I actually liked him, something I can't say for many others. Most relationships, I've jumped into bed with them, basing my feelings solely on sex and very little else. With him it was different, and I think this is why it feels so fucking painful.

He's explained to me, he has realised he doesn't want kids. I mean, that would have come in handy on the first date when I well and truly laid my cards on the table. Some people might think it too much to ask someone if they want kids on the first date, but fuck it, time is of the essence and I didn't want to find myself in, well, this situation a few months down the line when I'd invested in something. Does it take dating me to realise you never want to procreate? Or is it actually something else? Who knows, but if I do put the male human race off procreating, maybe I should start doing talks in schools as some sort of contraception – no doubt it'll stop many unwanted teen pregnancies.

Where do I go from here? Well, currently, absolutely nowhere. I've got the Rona and have been forced to stay in my flat, staring at the same four walls for the past five days now. I appear to have completed Netflix, iPlayer, and Amazon Prime, and I have nothing worth eating left in the house. Imagine an unwashed, crazy-looking cavewoman, and you're close to how I look right now. Work keeps me busy, yes, it also has the ability to drive me to the depths of despair, but right now, I could really do with occupying my time. This does not include crying over pictures and videos of us or constantly checking if he's on WhatsApp so he can take back everything he's said and tell me he can't possibly live without me.

Seriously, why do I do this to myself? What is it in us that tells us this is what we want, because I'm not sure I signed up for multiple heartbreaks. In no Disney film do the princesses get shat on or find out Prince Charming is actually a massive cunt. I appreciate showing children the sort of relationships I've endured may actually stop evolution in it tracks, but some real life would have been pretty handy.

I read an article the other day that explained half of women born in 1990 have not had a child by their thirtieth birthday; enter me. What bugs me isn't this fact – actually, I'd like to find these other soul sisters and give them a high five – it's the fact that there's an article about it. I get that they're writing and saying, 'Oh, it's perfectly fine not to have a baby by the time you're thirty,' but it's backhanded. It's a bit like when a man streaked naked at a football match: they didn't film it because, in essence, that's what he wanted – attention. So, by constantly giving attention to this conversation, it's actually doing the opposite of what's intended.

Instead of talking about what people aren't doing, why don't we talk about what they are? Have an article saying, 'Half of the women born in 1990 are independent badasses that are choosing themselves instead of society's fucked-up plan for them,' or words to that effect. Don't get me wrong – my friends with kids are the ultimate badasses, but just because I've not pushed anything out of my vagina doesn't mean I'm just an ass.

But here I am, dusting myself off again and preparing myself for the conversation around my lack of relationship. This possibly has to be the shortest relationship I've ever been in, officially only lasting a month and a half from when he asked me to be his girlfriend. No matter how many heartbreaks I go through, I ultimately always go back to the point of finding that right fit.

Maybe he wasn't that for me, but at least he was guiding me in the right direction. If they get better every time, the next one's bound to be great, even if they're just a great step up.

Valentines 2022

I thought this Valentine's was going to be different. Instead, I'm alone once more in my flat, surrounded by memories of what could have been, what I feel should have been. With only a card from my 'wife' wishing me a Happy Galentine's day.

'Another year, another nob head, another trip to the clinic.'

Thankfully for us, a trip to the clinic only involves at-home vaginal swabs. I'm not sure if I could take the in-person judgement of me yet again re-entering the clinic to say that yes, I yet again failed at another relationship. What appears to hurt the most is that this isn't how I saw this ending. I thought this would be my happy ending. But instead, I'm here, having demolished two tubs of ice cream, trying to fill the void he has left. The unanswered questions, the longing to go back in time to when this felt so right.

I'm back to having to get used to the Saturday night scaries, the Sunday scaries, and everything in between. Thankfully I've learnt a lot since I was last in this position. Previously I would be jumping on the next half-eligible man in sight. But who would I attract in the state I'm in? Not anyone I'd want to be with, that's for sure. I don't want to be with me right now, so why would I expect anyone else to be?

I'm often faced with sadness recently, but frankly, I'm not

sure where this stems from. Is it the loss of my ex-boyfriend? The loss of my current, now ex-boyfriend No Drama, who I saw a spark of light and a future with? Was I just blindsided, or did he feel what I felt? On talking to my therapist, I established that I don't believe you can be in love with someone without them feeling the same. I was falling in love for the first time in what felt like a lifetime. I was letting someone in, I was accepting kindness where I had only ever accepted drama. That's the thing – I told him I can't speak to him because I'm hurting, and he's actually listened! No man has ever actually respected my wishes, which makes this all the more painful. He was kind, he was respectful, he was mine.

It's so much easier when there's drama, when someone steals your car, takes drugs or cheats on you. There's an obvious line that's been crossed. But this? What even is this type of break-up, how do I grieve this? However much I want to slag him off to make this whole thing seem more understandable, I can't.

Where do I go from here? I don't know. All I know is when they say, 'It's better to have loved and lost than not loved at all,' I finally get it. Because this start to love was healthy, it was kind, and it was calm. I now know that this love is out there, even if it's not with who I thought.

I will always be grateful to him for showing me this, however painful losing it is.

Mirror image

When I look in the mirror, what do I see? My worth. From a young age, I felt my worth was defined by my appearance, not my kindness, not my personality, and certainly not my brains. I was never particularly academic, so to be defined by this would ultimately be a failure. I struggled to make friends and felt overwhelmed in large groups, so I was never going to be valued for my personality. I tried to be kind but was painfully shy, and people overwhelmed me.

Being the youngest, I felt overlooked, overshadowed by the successes or struggles of those who went before me. If one of my siblings was good at something, I felt it pointless to try as I would never live up to their standard. If they were struggling with mental illness, I felt my own mental health struggles weren't as bad as theirs and was even once told by a doctor that I was trying to copy my sister when I expressed my depression.

Growing up in a big family, I often felt invisible. Everyone seemed to speak a bit louder or perform a bit better. I'm sure, looking back, this was purely in my head, and I'm sure my siblings felt similar, if not the same, as me. People as a whole seem to think it was OK to compare us all the time; looking back, I feel that this really shaped who I was. If it wasn't family members, it was teachers, and ultimately this comparison became so ingrained in me that I still have it to this day.

I never seemed to get told how clever I was, but I remember time and time again being told how cute I was, how pretty I was, how innocent I looked. Maybe that was part of being the youngest; don't get me wrong, I was also told how annoying I was and how embarrassing I was. I think I learnt early on that if I was slim and pretty, all the other problems and struggles I had wouldn't be so bad.

I was thirty-one years old before I was diagnosed as having an eating disorder. I couldn't believe the words being said to me. I wasn't underweight, and I didn't resemble a skeleton, so how could I have an eating disorder? I told myself for a long time I had disordered eating; this was my safety net. When I was using, I was thin and grey, or heroin chic, and I thought I looked the best I ever had but could probably still do with losing half a stone. When I first went into rehab, I began binging and, ultimately, throwing up. Over the years, I've weighed food, calorie counted, only eaten from a child's plate or given up food entirely. What I've come to learn is that it's not how you look that determines whether or not you have an eating disorder, but the thoughts in your mind.

In recovery, it's very easy for someone to declare they're not a drug addict because they didn't end up homeless, they didn't go to prison, or they maintained a full-time job. Yet, from the outside, if you're taking any drug on a daily basis, regardless of your situation, you are still, in fact, a drug addict. This works with food, too; just because you're not visually unwell doesn't mean your mind isn't unwell, and that is how we hide it.

But where does the answer lie? Where do I go from here? I want to keep this all a secret, my late-night binges, my constant calorie counting, my constant judgements on my appearance. I feel that without them, I will somehow be exposed, yet I'm hurting myself by doing all this.

Who would I be without all these habits? Well, my ultimate fear is of being fat, that this would somehow make my value go down. Like I'm an old car being sold on a parking lot, with every pound I gain, a new scratch or dent appears, making me less appealing than the shiny red car next to me. Society's expectations have not helped, and I myself have said, 'If I am to be single and childless, the least I can do is look hot in the process.' Unfortunately, my expectation of 'hot' is at the top of a mountain I can never reach. I will never be thin enough, pretty enough, or even just enough. Not for other people, but for me.

The number on the scales tells a story, and much like my reflection in the mirror, it is not one of worth – it is one of lies. I don't see myself how other people see me, and I don't see myself as how I am. Deep down, I know the outside stuff is unimportant; if you're a good person, this will shine through. Unfortunately, looking at myself, I probably would come to the assumption that I'm not a good person either.

I don't have the answer to where I go from here. I don't know how to find balance and how to not be constantly plagued by the idea of other people getting in the way of my control around food. What I do know is I can't let it control me. It's funny how I'm not actually controlling anything – it is, in fact, controlling me.

Facing fears

If I've learnt one thing in these last six months, it is that life is precious. So many times, I've put off doing something for another time. I'll climb that mountain when I'm stronger, I'll publish the book when I'm a better writer, I'll start loving myself when I'm thinner. The list is endless. My support bubble through lockdown knew me pretty well, and she knew my fears, well, most of them. We happened to be watching a documentary on caves, and in a passing comment, she asked if I liked them. 'Fuck no' or words to that effect was the answer she got. On Christmas Day 2020, I opened a voucher to find she'd bought us an experience to go into a cave trampolining near Snowdon; it's safe to say I was terrified.

I had been getting better at facing my fears; I'd even walked over the odd dodgy bridge on many of our walks. We decided to climb Snowdon whilst we were there, but at this point had no real idea when we might be allowed to go. But at last, the weekend away had arrived, finally free to climb a mountain and shit myself in a cave. I was in need of the fresh air, the challenge, to just have my walking boots on and walk until I could walk no more.

My sister had recommended a book to me after Prince Charming's death called *Chase the Rainbow* by Poorna Bell. Before reading this, I have to say I still had a large amount of anger towards him, I hate to admit it, but I even blamed him for my latest break-up. I finally felt like I was on the right path, and I felt he had somehow come and fucked it all up. Grief can make you feel a hundred different emotions in a matter of minutes. This book was the comfort blanket I needed. Poorna had lost her husband to suicide; her book is frank and painfully beautiful, and one I think everyone should read. Her compassion was infectious. I went from feeling such anger to such love, such sadness, such empathy for the man who had felt so desperate.

I decided to email her, not for a response, not for anything, really. I just wanted to let her know how much her book had helped me. Helped me see the human in him again and not be angry at him for things that weren't his doing. As I sat in a cafe at the bottom of Snowdon, really not having a clue what I'd let myself in for, I received an email back. Never in a million years had I expected a response – or at best, I thought I'd get an auto-generated one, but I didn't really think I deserved even that. She was so kind, so compassionate for the pain I was feeling, that I began to cry into my coffee. I felt a release, a release from all the anger. In all honesty, I think I'd prefer to feel angry; it keeps me from feeling sad. If I was angry, it didn't hurt as much, but I needed to let go; this anger wasn't for him.

With the email still imprinted in my mind, I faced a fear I hadn't realised I was facing. I was not only going to face my fear of heights but also my fear of grieving. I hadn't really taken into account what walking up a mountain involved. There I was, standing so close to the sky I couldn't look down. I was so grateful for my newly purchased walking poles, the ones I always believed were for old people; without them, I wouldn't have made it up this mountain. Apparently, if you're scared of heights, mountains may be a bit of a challenge.

At times I freaked out, I froze, I was scared to move, but I made it. I felt utter elation from reaching the top of Snowdon and seeing the beauty of it covered in snow. Being so close to the sky felt so important; it's where I believe all the ones we have lost live, and it was a feeling of closeness I will never forget. Peace came over me, and for the first time in months, I felt a sense of calm. Life will throw us curveballs, take us through some fucked-up situations, and at times our hearts may feel like they will never recover.

The following day I may as well have skipped into that cave. What is fear anyway? What the fuck am I so scared of? I've spent my life being scared, scared that people don't like me, that I will be judged, that I'll fall down a very flat hill and die, or be pushed off a bridge. So far, none of these irrational fears has ever amounted to anything, nothing bad has ever happened. If I spent less time worrying about what might happen, I might, in fact, have the chance to live this beautiful thing called life.

The people around us, the love you receive from strangers, the email from someone who knows the pain you're going through: these are our walking poles. They are what offer us stability on what feels like an impossible road. We may think we appear stronger without them, but why try and be strong when you can be carried?

Maurice Pierre

My darling boy is four today, I dread to think how my life would have been the last four years without him. My four-legged fur baby has brought more joy to my life than ever imaginable. Dogs truly are the best therapy. Their constant company, the comfort, even just their presence has made such a massive difference in my life.

Before I got him, I remember so many people trying to put me off the idea. I had gotten my first dog Ruby when I was 19 years old, so in many people's eyes, I'd had a constant tie in my adult life. To me, they are not a tie, they are the glue that sticks me back together. Yes, you have to consider them in everything you do. I never make a decision without him in mind, whether it's holidays or dating or, in fact, the man I'm dating. Seeing how someone is with him tells me a lot about a potential suitor and has put me off a good many of them!

However much I've tried to hold onto a young lifestyle, in all honesty, I live like I have a dog. I love my home comforts, I love walking, and there are not many places I like going that aren't dog friendly. To me, he saved me. I had gone from having a boyfriend and a dog to nothing, my home felt so empty, so quiet, and he was by far the best thing I could have done for myself.

Every morning, he is pleased to see me, regardless of my mood, what I'm wearing or how much sleep I've had. The pure joy I see on his face when we're out walking could melt any bad mood I'm in, and when I've needed comfort, he's snored loudly in my ear as I've acted as the big spoon.

He marks a time in my life when things changed, I chose to live, I chose to choose myself and wake up and face the world.

He will never be an inconvenience, a tie, or a burden to me. He is my family. Whilst my friends have children and partners, I have him by my side.

I will be eternally grateful to this smelly, wonky-toothed farting dog for being my rainbow in the storm. What is a tie to one person is another's reason for living.

More pain, more gain

What makes a love story? Is it the happily ever after? More often than not, it's the fight people go through to get to love. We're often shown the chaos that comes with love, the drama, so is it any surprise that's what we're drawn to?

It's been just over a week since No Drama contacted me again, declaring he made a mistake, that he missed me, and that he'd do whatever to make our relationship work. I spent most of the week leading up to it in a state of anxiety. Could this finally be what I'd been waiting for? Had I grieved enough now that I could finally have my happy ever after?

I was advised by my therapist to stay away from playing the victim and allowing him to take complete blame, and to meet him as an equal. After all, we're all human and we all make mistakes. I'm not going to lie, I myself felt I'd been a fucking delight. Aside from the untimely death of Prince Charming and struggling to know who I should be reassuring, I really tried to make that relationship work. However, I'm all for taking advice so I went to meet him with an open heart and wanted to sort out what I thought was the one that got away.

What I was greeted with was far from the person who had sent me the message pouring out their heart. It felt like I'd dragged him there, that he wanted to be anywhere but with me. When I asked how he was feeling he replied 'unstable'. Yes, a massive red flag, but me being me, I wanted to give him the benefit of the doubt. I tried to understand why I was there, and I wanted to find the person who had poured his heart out to me. Where was he? Had someone else sent this message?

At this point, I was feeling pretty insecure and felt like I was the one trying to convince him to be with me. Because of this, I became overly affectionate and kissed him. Was I trying to kiss this frog into a prince? Perhaps. Unfortunately, my attempts didn't work, and what unfolded was definitely more frog than prince. He said, 'I've got to be honest with you about something.' When someone says this to me in the future, I may run for the hills or hide under a rock. My heart sank.

He went on to tell me that since we'd split up, he'd gotten back in contact with his ex; she had reached out to him because she was having a hard time. This was the same ex that had hurt him so much that he'd gotten scared of our relationship. I felt physically sick. I'd love to be one of those people that this wouldn't bother, but it does. He went on to say that they had agreed they didn't want any relationship getting in the way of their friendship. What the actual fuck? Is this how people win you back these days? What's more, they were seeing each other once in the week, once at the weekend, so potentially more than we would even see each other. I'm all for having amicable break-ups, being able to say hello without wanting to punch each other in the face, but this... this was too much. He tried to convince me they were purely friends and even said if it was more, why would he have asked me here! I was starting to wonder that myself because, frankly, this was a pretty pitiful way to try to win someone back!

Pushing back the tears, I tried to stay calm and just told him that this made me feel quite insecure; I was longing for the man I thought I'd been falling in love with to reappear. I said, 'That wasn't what I expected you to say,' and he asked me what I thought he was going to say. I replied, 'I thought you were going to tell me you'd slept with someone else'... deadly silence. I'm now winded and find myself asking the question I really don't want to hear the answers to. My worst fears were, of course, confirmed, and all this in the space of five minutes. What the fuck has just happened and why the fuck did he want me here!?

I wanted to run, I wanted to get out of there as soon as I could, but I'd already agreed to go for a drink. Of course, I could have changed my mind, but I was really hoping the man who poured his heart out to me, saying he wanted to be a team, to be lovers, would fucking reappear.

He didn't. And made a very half-arsed attempt to win me back. He told me I should think about if I could deal with all this, like it was normal. Of course, this made me think I was having an adverse reaction to something in my gut that felt so wrong. HE messaged me, HE wanted me back, HE wanted to meet. I was finally turning a corner, and he just came in, poured his heart out, and made me dream again only to trample on it, have a piss on it, and set fire to it. How had I gotten this so wrong AGAIN?

I had an emergency therapy session; this just wasn't making sense. I needed to speak to someone who wasn't one of my friends – who were all calling him a massive cunt – and see if I had somehow done something wrong, or if I should be OK with this. He'd sent me a few messages telling me how nice it was to see me and quickly backtracked from almost everything he'd said to me... enter more mind-fuckery.

Now the old me, the one before therapy, before

establishing boundaries and a small amount of self-worth, would have gone along with all this just to get the slightest glimpse of love. But this wasn't love; this was unstable, and it was only going to lead me to more pain. Having asked him to try to work out what he wanted and leaving the ball completely in his court, ready to take a shot at my heart at any moment, it dawned on me, where was my ball?

My ball was safely with me, by my side and not willing to play tennis with him. I messaged him with what little self-worth I had left and said, 'I know what I want, and it's not someone who can't work out who to put first, me or their ex.' For the first time in a long time, I'd found my worth, I don't want to come second to someone's ex. We all have pasts, me included, but I would never jeopardise my future for my past. I want to walk forwards and not back.

Camino 2022

I don't think I've ever needed some time out so much in my life. I'm finally going back walking, back to where I left off in hope that I can find myself again. The strong woman I've become. No matter how many times I go away alone, I still get the fear that I'm not capable. I arrived in Spain to a snowstorm, and with very little Spanish vocabulary, no matter how much I have tried to learn the language over the past few years, I always end up sounding like one of the Mitchel brothers.

After about four hours, I finally arrive in Estella. Even on the different buses, I was never completely sure that they understood where I was trying to get to. Driving on the winding roads covered in snow, all I could do was pray that I was going to get to where I needed to be. Thankfully by some small miracle, I arrived and managed to find the hostel I was to stay in, which I had last stayed in four years previously.

The one thing I both love and hate about these sorts of trips is that you need to talk to people. Some people you quite frankly would want to run away from. I found my bed and in that moment realised once again I was all alone. A few people in my dorm made small talk, but one stuck out. She asked if I wanted to go for dinner and I jumped at the chance, not wanting to eat on my own.

This woman turned out to be someone who carried me through this walk. Neither of us had expected to walk with one another, or anyone for that matter, but we seemed to just click. It's very rare to find someone who is on your level, let alone someone you can walk with for seven days straight. Often you meet people that are like emotional vampires and won't stop talking, but we seemed to find what we needed in each other. Companionship and support. I would say eighty per cent of the time, we didn't actually talk, we just walked, sometimes together and sometimes at a distance, but we were there for one another.

We supported each other through blisters, pain, tears and laughter. I truly believe that you find people you are meant to, and I was definitely meant to meet this guardian angel.

A week on the Camino can feel like a lifetime, and it felt like we had worked through a lifetime of grief together. I didn't want to leave, I didn't want to go back to reality. I wanted to just walk. But if I've learnt anything over the years, it's that you can't constantly run away from your problems; you have to face them. I had faced a lot on this Camino, and it was time I went back and started trying at life again.

Before I went away, someone I had been friends with for over a decade had told me he had feelings for me. Going back meant facing this, facing the possibility that a friendship could be something more. It was complicated; he had been also friends with Prince Charming and had been my rock over the last few months. Had our love and grief for Prince Charming brought us together? Could it work?

My Camino amiga had simply told me to go for it. She explained if I never take a chance, I will never know. Our friendship could be ruined, or it could be everything we've ever wanted.

The Best Friend

Growing up, it has been instilled in me that you should fall in love with your best friend. Over the years, I've had many a complicated friendship, with one side ultimately always getting hurt. What if that didn't always have to happen?

Ok, this is complicated, or sensitive, as my therapist calls it. We are, in fact, the only two people complicating it. I have seen this man crying, laughing, setting fire to toilet paper shoved up his arsehole, and with many, many new women and girlfriends. I have seen his highs, his lows and everything in between. In all honesty, I never got it. By it, I mean him. I loved him as my friend and, ultimately, as Prince Charming's friend, but I never understood the attraction and attention he got, and he got a lot. Was it simply just that I was in a relationship, that I couldn't see him in that way?

I would see him with attractive woman after attractive woman, and it always puzzled me. He was great, he was fun, and yes, he was attractive, but he was sensitive, and openly so, and I guess it made me feel uncomfortable in some way. I'd never met anyone who was so openly in touch with his feelings, I was used to having to dig for them.

Fast forward ten-plus years... Prince Charming has died, he's left not only me but him, and we seem to have found each other through our grief. Am I being disloyal? Would he be angry? Upset? Or would he be happy I'm falling for someone he too loved and respected? Do our feelings for each other somehow cancel the feelings we had for him?

My therapist asked whose guilt it was that I was feeling; in all honesty, I'm not sure. After going to see the body of someone whom I loved and still do, this best friend drove to me and slept on my sofa, so I didn't have to be alone. At no point over the past four years since the relationship ended has he ever given me any impression that we would ever be more than just friends. After months of comforting me as I grieved, and whilst I moaned about yet another relationship breakdown, he was there, not slimy, not hitting on me, just there.

For the first time in over a decade, he told me that there was more than friendship between us. To say I was shocked was frankly the biggest fucking understatement. So many questions went through my head for the next week. I was desperate not to lose this man who I so loved, but with a chance that he could be what I dreamed of my whole life. Could I, in fact, fall in love with my best friend?

The chicken and the egg

It's hard to know what came first, the eating disorder or my digestive problems. For as long as I can remember, I've suffered with various different digestive problems. I've been poked, prodded and medicated more times than I care to remember. Did this create the eating disorder or did the eating disorder create the digestive problems?

I've been told to cut food groups out, I've stopped eating at times for fear of feeling unwell, taken laxatives to cure the bloating, even made myself sick when the pain became too much to bear. Is it any wonder this has led to an eating disorder?

On the outside, the mask shows someone who is carefree, comfortable in her naked body, even revels in it. Behind the mask is someone who obsessively weighs themselves, tries to count calories all day in her head, and binges like a secret drug addict. Those binges ultimately turn to being sick or to laxatives.

My therapist told me how food was not really my problem, but love. I crave it like I crave food, often eating up as much love as I can only to feel unworthy of it and need rid of it as soon as possible. I'm what they call ambivalent attached, both anxious and avoidant, which reflects in my relationship with food.

The self-loathing I feel now is unimaginable; I've just binged on food and dropped those little pills like they would rid me of the guilt of eating. What it actually does is make me hate myself for yet again interfering with my body and somehow expecting the problem to go away. Every day I try to start again. I can do this on my own, I don't need help. I get scared that if I out this, I will lose control, but how much control do I actually have? I've not felt this out of control in a long time, and being aware of it makes it even harder. When you know you've got a problem, it's so much harder to ignore; it seems to be mocking me. It's like a devil on my shoulder laughing at me when I yet again fail.

How can I do this to myself time and time again, tell myself that I don't deserve love, from myself or anyone? Only the other day, I had convinced myself that things weren't going to work out with The Best Friend, only to uncover that it got in the way of my secret. The problem is that you come clean to people, and for a minute, it feels better, but if you don't continuously out yourself, are you lying or being dishonest?

Maybe it's an after-effect of grief, maybe it was something else, or maybe I've been hiding it from everyone and myself for a long time. I remember getting into what I thought were phases, on and off throughout my life. It was usually when I lived alone or I was alone because it was easier to cover up. But now I can't cover it up from myself, it's staring me straight in the face. Part of me is scared to surrender, to ask for help, because no doubt I will get fat. But if I don't ask for help, I'm not being authentic, and I don't want that either.

When I look in the mirror, I seem to see someone nobody else sees. I see the rolls, the curves in the wrong places. I see someone who could do better. Where is that balance between accepting oneself but also being healthy? I know going to the gym helps me to cope, I know eating good healthy food, in moderation, helps. Not exercising, eating chocolate, and being left to my own devices is a recipe for disaster. I can't be minded, though; I need to mind myself. Learn to love myself and accept that love without putting a guard up to stop it seeping in.

I'm exhausted from hating myself. If I put half as much time and energy into loving myself and accepting love, surely I would be OK, better than OK.

This is 32

So, it has become abundantly clear that my life has not panned out how I or anyone around me had hoped. I've cried over more men than I thought humanly possible, gotten over a drug addiction, and at present, my eating disorder is being dealt with as best I can. The first step is admitting there is a problem, and I, for one, don't want to let it control me. It appears I have been fighting to control some part of my life for so long that this is what has reared its ugly head.

I spent the day with The Best Friend, a man who has shown up for me when I have needed him the most. He has let me cry on him through my grief and has been supporting me while I try to conquer this next part of my life, all the while being kind and making me laugh when he can. He made me breakfast and took me to Monkey World. I am just a big kid, trying to fake it as an adult most of the time. It poured down with rain as it often does on my birthday, but he was like the sun shining in through the clouds. How has this happened? How have I found someone who is my best friend and who I now appear to be falling in love with?

It's said that love finds you when you least expect it, and that appears to be true. I have to admit in the years after my break-up with Prince Charming I did try it on with him a few times, desperate for a night of passion, no strings attached. I even nibbled his ear once and embarrassingly pretty much begged him to sleep with me. I always got a no. This only led me to believe I must repulse him, he always said he wouldn't out of loyalty to Prince Charming. I didn't buy it, no man I have ever encountered had this amount of morals, so I concluded that he just didn't see me like that. Turns out some men do have morals, and this quality is one that has made me feel so safe with him.

I finished my day by meeting up with my best girlfriends, my ride-or-dies; these women have really shown up when I've needed them. With each year I'm slowly getting more comfortable with them mixing with each other. Maybe it is because I am finally seeing that I am worthy of not only romantic love, but friendship love as well.

Thirty-two is getting matching tattoos with my friend, spending the day with a friend who has become so much more, and being around people who love me when I cannot love myself. This year may not have started how I had hoped, but through being carried by those I love dearly, I know that none of this is a setback. It is, in fact, a plot twist, one that leads me to where I'm meant to be.

You're going to die soon

I'm sitting in picturesque Malaga, with my sister on my second holiday abroad this year so far. I have a great job, albeit busy and often demanding. I have a beautiful flat and am currently having my courtyard redone. I have far too many clothes in my wardrobe and what appears to be an adoring boyfriend at home who is also one of my best friends. And all I can think about is FAT.

I've wasted so many years of my life feeling like I'm not good enough, if I were thinner, posher, less posh, richer, poorer, shorter, taller, the list goes on and on. My sister, unfortunately, has felt the same, and she told me how she snaps out of it, even if for a moment. She tells herself she's going to die soon. I laughed at this dramatic statement, but she is right. Even now, having experienced great loss recently, all I can think about is fat.

The joke of it is I know I'm not fat, but some arsehole in my head likes to tell me I am. I remember being referred to as 'big boned' as a child, a comment I've held onto for dear life. The thing about being 'big boned' is you can't reduce your bone mass, so as far as my younger self and the arsehole in my head think, I will forever be 'big boned'. Again, I'm not how I was described; the more common notion is I am petite, lean, athletic, yet I don't seem to be able to accept any of these and cling to a comment made two decades ago.

The thing is, I could die soon. Thankfully, there is no actual sign of that happening, I've still got a lot of shit I want to do. However, one of those things I want to do is to not spend my life thinking that I'm not good enough. If I think about all the time I've wasted, I will surely have a heart attack. We have been conditioned to think that people that are full of themselves are the enemy, when actually they are the aim. I would love nothing more than myself and everyone around be to be full of themselves, to love themselves, to cherish every minute they have on this earth as if they were going to die soon. Why does it take a near-death experience or something drastic to shake us the fuck up?

Tomorrow we are going on the Caminito del Rey, a hike that frankly looks pretty shady. When googling the hike, a related search came up 'deaths on the Caminito del Rey', hardly helping with my fear of heights. But fuck it, as the young ones say, 'YOLO', or 'You only live once' to people not born in Gen Z. Tomorrow, when I'm trying not to fall down a canyon, I will surely not be thinking about FAT, I will be hoping and praying that the cushioning on my arse stops me from dying when I fall.

No doubt I will contemplate my fat again and again, but I will keep reminding myself 'I'm going to die soon.'

The two faces of love

Growing up, I was shown two very different faces of love. One kind, nurturing and caring, the other controlling, manipulative and cold. As far as I knew, the two came as a set, and one was not possible without the other.

My many failed relationships mirrored these qualities and, for a time, made me feel safe, as it was all I ever knew. If someone had these qualities, I was drawn to them like a moth to a flame. I would forever make excuses for the cold side of them, and gush about how lovely they COULD be. When people saw the cruel side, I would do everything to convince them that that wasn't really who they were, if only you knew the person I knew.

I've never been able to see that I was in a vicious cycle that would lead me to more hurt and upset. That and the never-ending feeling that you were in some way a disappointment. Even writing this is hard, to actually put pen to paper, or fingers to keyboard. How can two faces of love belong to one person, and for that person to not only be unaware but also not intend to make you feel this way?

Tonight, I had a breakthrough, a new awareness, a light was shone on this dark secret I appear to keep within my heart. I no longer want to look for these two faces of love, I don't want to pass on these two faces of love, and I certainly don't want to become these two faces of love. All very possible, if I myself don't break this cycle.

So, with that in mind, my therapist set me a task, a task of self-love and letting go. It's a full moon and the summer solstice is just around the corner. My courtyard has just been finished and my small fire pit has been put in its new place. I start writing the qualities I wish to die and let go of, the main one being 'love with two faces'. I then write a list of things I want to welcome into my life, mainly 'accepting love that is calm and consistent', words that would not describe my exes. I sit cross-legged facing the fire, rollie in my mouth with my personal anthem 'Following the Sun' playing into my headphones.

I fold up the list of things I want to die, and set it alight, watching as the flames engulf the words I've written. It seems to burn out quickly. I start playing the song again, but this time set alight the things I want to keep. Maybe it's how I folded it or set fire to it, but the paper starts to resemble a flower, a blossoming flower. I watch this burn, even having to start the song for a third time. I shut my eyes and pray, pray that these intentions grace me, pray that this small ritual somehow alleviates some of the pain and suffering that has been etched on my heart. I leave it up to the moon, the sun, and the stars above to change my narrative once and for all.

With each new breath I take, there is a chance for me to change my path. It's time for a rebirth, a new chance at life and love. The love with one face, the love that is, in fact, just love.

Three's a crowd

Or maybe it doesn't have to be. I'm faced with, quite frankly, my worst nightmare, three men I've dated in one place. One is my boyfriend, one I slept with and spent a long time obsessing over, and one didn't even make it past the start line. There are 11 people at this birthday BBQ, so basically, I've dated a third of them.

Most people I've dated in the past would have taken great umbrage in having to deal with other people I've dated; they'd get possessive and jealous and cause a scene in any way they could. He didn't, we were able to laugh and joke about this awkward situation we found our-selves in and, well, not make it awkward.

It's been my pattern to be drawn to men that don't value me, that don't pick me first, and that make me question how they feel, and one of these men was here. I could feel myself wanting to slip back into this familiarity, the familiar unease, the anxiousness I had become so accustomed to. But there was my best friend, the man I had fallen deeply in love with, who has my back in all situations, looking into my eyes, reminding me that safety was my new place of comfort.

It's only been a short while since we officially got together, although it feels like a lot longer. He has been in the back-ground for over a decade; he has had my back even when I haven't been aware. He makes me laugh until my sides hurt and never makes me question his love or loyalty. Frankly, this feels fucking uncomfortable, this is new territory I'm dealing with. To find a man that is able to make a joke out of the fact his girlfriend has dated a third of a party and hold his own is quite incredible. He said to me that it is not his doing; because he trusts me implicitly and feels so secure, I am allowing him to be like this. We are a team, there is no one that is better than the other.

When he annoys me, I tell him, when I'm scared of something, I tell him, when something triggers me, I tell him, and we work it out together. We don't keep things bottled up and wait for an explosion; we both put one hundred per cent into our relationship because we want it to work. We've seen the error of our ways and together we want to build something that is going to last.

If you told me six months ago I would be planning weddings and babies, firstly, I'd want to know who the fuck with! Life can change in a moment, that much I've been taught time and time again. I'm constantly questioning whether I'm getting carried away, whether I'm going insane, but I have never felt so calm as I do when I'm with him.

I look back on the relationships I've had, the times I thought I was in love; he has made me realise once again what love is. I loved Prince Charming, but if I'm completely honest with myself and my heart, I haven't loved anyone since him, until now. I didn't know any of the others; I had imagined who they were in my head, so desperate to find 'the one' and someone who loved me, I filled in the gaps in an attempt to create a happily ever after. I know this man, I've seen him cry, I've seen him laugh and I've seen him dramatise many a situation. When I look into his eyes, I see safety, I see what love is, I see what kindness is.

I really hope I don't come back to my writing and say that this hasn't worked out. I don't see a way that it won't, as long as I don't get in the way of this love that I've come to realise I really deserve. He is my best friend, my partner in crime, my love and my safety. I may have had to travel through some pretty shitty places to get here, but without them, we wouldn't have found each other.

The friend whose birthday it was told me how he didn't believe in fate or that things were written in the stars. But if he did, he would very much think that we were, in fact, the fate that people talk of.

How to be in a relationship

All my attention up until now has been fully focused on how to be single, how to be independent, and how to be OK with being alone. Now finally being in a relationship with neither a drug addict nor sociopath, I seem to have forgotten how to actually be in a relationship.

For the past few years, I've been parenting myself, teaching myself how to put air in tyres, how to survive the Sunday scaries, and if I'm honest, part of me feels like I'm turning my back on that woman warrior. Part of me, believe it or not, feels like I've failed by getting into a relationship, that I should be happy living the life of a single woman and carry that crown for all to see.

This has a lot to do with people's innate obsession with pairing everyone up. Part of me wants to rebel against the norm and tell them all to fuck off. However, there also has been this longing in myself to meet my mate, my partner in crime, and, God forbid, have a family in the country I always talked about. Enter… man who lives in the country who happens to be one of my best friends and wants all of that too. How awful!

So here I am, with everything I've ever wished before me, and for some reason, I don't know what to do with it. Please don't get me wrong, we have our hurdles to jump, and unfortunately, one of them is me. It appears I've not made it either past the honeymoon period or the completely insane period in quite some time. I was 19 years old when I last crossed over this line, and now at 32, I feel a little out of my depth.

I've spent a long time getting to know myself, getting to know the patterns that I used to follow that were more than a little destructive, having a lot of therapy and crying on numerous friends and their babies, but it appears I haven't learnt what it takes to be in a relationship.

One of the most unfortunate lessons is admitting when you're wrong. No one likes to do this, least of all me. But last night, I appear to have created an argument for no real reason; was I sabotaging? We had just had a lovely weekend together. We'd had dinner with my friends, something I have never done previously, one, because I didn't really have friends, and two, because my exes never wanted to socialise with my friends. Then we spent the next day enjoying the sun in the countryside and I took his Land Rover for a ride. All lovely, wholesome and beautiful!

He made one passing comment about my friend, and later he felt too tired for sex, and from that I managed to turn it into him not wanting to have sex with me, me feeling rejected, and me not coping with dividing my time between him and my friends. Now who's dating the crazy person? I was hysterical, uncontrollably sobbing. We had had sex earlier that day, he had showed me love and affection all day, told me how hot I was, so where the fuck did this come from?

Has the crazy finally rubbed off on me, or was it always there? Now I know I'm not crazy, just slightly challenging at times, but after some serious work, I have come to the realisation I am just a person who's been through her fair share of car crashes, literally, and sometimes doesn't have the tools to deal with situations. It might be prudent to add I'm also trying to come off the anti-psychotics prescribed to me thirteen years ago whilst in rehab, so this may also have played a part.

For thirteen years I never questioned the drugs I was put on, I almost used their diagnosis of bipolar and depression as a crutch to explain why I was the way I was. More often than not the person I was in a relationship with would jump on that too, to explain why I was angry when they hadn't come home and hadn't told me where they were. But recently I have questioned it for the first time and have chosen to come off the drugs and finally feel completely me. I may be more insane, or I may be seeing things clearly for the first time, and with the help and support of everyone around me, I look forward to knowing exactly what feelings are mine.

This is not me advising people to come off drugs, well, not prescribed ones, at least! Is it any surprise when I entered rehab addicted to heroin, I was given this diagnosis? Is there anyone on the planet that wouldn't be depressed? For the first time in a very long time, or ever, I'm now in a relationship with someone who agrees – well, he did before last night! Although this may be a bumpy road, learning how to be in a healthy relationship as well as not being on any prescribed medication, I know he'll be along for the ride.

I will continue to make mistakes and learn from them, I will continue to sometimes sabotage what I have always wanted. However, I know over time, this will become less and less, and I know I will continue to strive for what I know I deserve, and I will feel strong in my convictions. But most of all, I will hold my hands up when I'm wrong and not just say sorry but show that I'm trying not to behave the way I once felt was protecting me.

Adult

Here I find myself in my flat alone, but it's different. I have no Ben and Jerry's, no chocolate, or any other food to binge on to fill the void I once felt. I no longer feel the despair I once did. My dog is sitting by my side, still acting as my constant comfort blanket. I'm finally in a relationship with myself. Yes, I'm in a relationship with a man also, but the one I'm now in with myself is far more important because without that, there wouldn't be any other relationship.

My closing off this chapter in my life was never about meeting someone, it was about meeting myself and being OK with what I saw. Of course, I still have days when I don't like what I see, I'm human, and today was one of them. The difference is I didn't come home this evening and feel like harming myself, I didn't reach for the food, which I would ultimately find ways to get rid of in a matter of minutes. I didn't seek attention from another man because I've barely had contact with my boyfriend all day. I haven't felt the need to have contact with my boyfriend all day, because I know I'M OK.

It's come to my attention that I've been stuck in a child state, constantly attracting people that feel the need to parent me, whether that be in romantic relationships or platonic. At times in my life, I've definitely needed this, but I don't anymore, I can parent myself. I don't have all the answers, but I will figure it out, I am capable of that, something I have never actually believed before. The thing is when you have these parental figures in your life that, in turn, like to 'look after you', it only feeds into your idea that you can't do it alone.

When I began writing this book, I was in need of much more than parenting. When I've read back through it, it only shows me how far I've come from the frankly pathetic child I was. I was stuck in my child, constantly needing the stabilisers just to cycle down the road. I've proved to myself, however wobbly it might become, I will always be able to get back up.

Never in a million years did I think I'd come off my medication; they were one of my many stabilisers, and another voice telling me I wasn't capable to survive alone. Ok, I'm not completely off them yet, but I've almost halved the high dose I was on, and I've survived. Painful stuff happens in life, relationships break up, people you love die, but we can survive it. We can use this pain as our strength, as ammo to live the best life we can.

Someone told me that all these challenges in life help create your story. I for one wouldn't want to watch a film where everything was just plain sailing, where's the fun in that? I look at people that seemed to have breezed through life, but they don't have the same substance as people that have had to get through hard times. Is it any real surprise that none of my girlfriends I hold so dear, who I call warrior women, have breezed through life? When we look for our idols, are they people that have had it easy or people that have fought tooth and nail for who they are and what they believe in?

No doubt there will be times when my eating disorder may re-appear, I may struggle with the appearance of the woman standing in front of me, I may go through more heartache, more grief, but that is this crazy, fucked-up thing they call life. With each of these challenges comes growth, comes more acceptance and more empathy for other people and myself.

Who knows where I will be in a month, a year, or five years? No one truly knows. All I know is with every day that passes, I am more equipped for what life may throw at me. I am in no way recovered, but I'm on the right path.

There still isn't anything in my fridge that resembles a meal, but for the first time in a really long time, I really want there to be.

Acknowledgments

To my parents, for getting me out of the gutter I found myself in and helping bring me back to life. To my mum, for teaching me the best things in life are free and being a role model for me. To my pops, for giving me my sense of humour and having faith in me when I didn't have faith in myself.

To my stepdad, for encouraging me in everything I do and taking me on, even in those *many* difficult years. To my stepmum, for being an example of a strong independent woman.

To my sisters, without you I would hate to think where I would be now. The love I have for each of you I could never put into words. Thank you for standing by me when no one else would, for picking me up when I was broken and for being my closest friends and confidants. I will be eternally grateful for having you in my life.

To my beautiful Paula, for showing me friendship is not about speaking all of the time but for always being there when I need you.

To Debbie, for putting up with me for the last thirteen years on a daily basis. I have probably spent more time with you than anyone I've been in a relationship with, and so far, you haven't asked for a divorce. For being by my side through the highs and the many lows. For putting up with "Anne" and guiding me when I was lost.

To Kate, for showing up when I needed you most, for

letting me be the lemon in your marriage and allowing me to come on your family holiday. For comforting me as I cried over *numerous* men and allowing me to be part of your family.

To Haley, for showing me how to be a strong independent woman, teaching me that I am capable of putting air in my tyres! For fuelling my sense of adventure and being an absolute rock to me. For being my support bubble in lockdown and carrying me through grief and craziness. For making me feel part of something.

To Tony and Sonya, for being my adoptive parents. For loving and supporting me in everything I do.

To my Lozza, for being there through my craziness and making me feel less alone.

To Victoria, for working with me for over one hundred sessions! For helping me find myself and encouraging me to be the best version of myself.

To Luke, for being my friend when I needed you the most. For showing me how a relationship can be and for loving me when I didn't know how to love myself. For not only embracing my independent side but for loving me because of it.

Lastly, to Rachael and all the beautiful souls at The Unbound Press, who without this wouldn't have been possible. Thank you for putting up with my many melt downs and for guiding and supporting me through this journey.

About the Author

Mariella Pearson took up writing in lock down, when her beloved dog had had enough of her taking him out on marathon walks, and realised that through her writing she could make other women like her feel less alone.

She's someone who is always up for an adventure. From her own experience, she knows how short and precious life is and this has given her the courage to experiment with new things; believing that everything is worth a try, even if it's just once!

Mariella loves to empower other women, and is always fascinated to learn more about how she operates, so she can be the best version of herself.

Her ability to laugh at herself through the chaos of life is infectious, helping us all to take life more lightly.

Ingram Content Group UK Ltd.
Milton Keynes UK
UKHW021813020723
424322UK00008B/45